Effective classroom management

This new edition of the successful and widely recommended *Effective Classroom Management* has been updated and restructured in the light of recent research and developments. It is written for new teachers and also for those who train or guide them while they gain experience, and combines practical advice on lesson organisation and teaching methods with an exploration of teachers' feelings about themselves and the children they teach.

Effective management in the classroom is discussed as a co-operative enterprise linked to classroom and school processes and the development of good relationships. It is considered from four aspects:

- *Management in the classroom* begins with four simple rules: get them in; get them out; get on with it; get on with them. The authors then give more detailed advice on analysing classroom organisation and reducing sources of friction.
- *Mediation with individuals* refers to knowledge of how to provide the counselling and guidance which some pupils require, understanding their problems and avoiding damaging confrontations in the classroom.
- *Modification of behaviour* involves applying learning theory to shaping and changing behaviour in ways which are practical and realistic within the routine of the normal classroom.
- *Monitoring school discipline* considers how schools evaluate the effectiveness of policies on discipline and how senior teachers can help colleagues cope with stress and other problems.

Colin J. Smith is Senior Lecturer in Education at the University of Birmingham, where he is tutor to courses for teachers of children with difficulties in learning. He is past editor of *Maladjustment and Therapeutic Education*, and has contributed widely to books and journals on special educational needs and discipline in schools. **Robert Laslett**, after some years of teaching in mainstream schools, worked in special schools until he was appointed as Lecturer in Education and Tutor to a course for teachers of children with emotional and behavioural difficulties. Following the publication of *Educating Maladjusted Children* he has written monographs for the Association of Workers for Children with Emotional and Behavioural Difficulties and the National Council for Special Education, and has contributed to books and journals on special educational needs.

Effective classroom management

A teacher's guide

Second edition

Colin J. Smith
and Robert Laslett

London and New York

First published 1993
by Routledge
11 New Fetter Lane, London EC4P 4EE

Simultaneously published in the USA and Canada
by Routledge
29 West 35th Street, New York, NY 10001

Reprinted 1993, 1995, 1996

© 1993 Colin J. Smith and Robert Laslett

Typeset in Palatino by
NWL Editorial Services, Langport, Somerset
Printed and bound in Great Britain by
Mackays of Chatham PLC, Chatham, Kent

British Library Cataloguing in Publication Data
A catalogue record for this book is available from the British Library

Library of Congress Cataloguing in Publication Data
A catalogue record for this book is available from the Library of Congress

ISBN 0-415-07152-6

Contents

Introduction

We have written this book particularly to help newly-qualified teachers establish and improve their classroom management. We hope that more experienced teachers, especially those charged with the task of acting as 'mentor' to new entrants to the profession, will also find this book useful as a means of organising reflection on their own experience of what makes teaching effective. Such teachers rarely have the time to examine and articulate the techniques which they have internalised over the years. We know that the first edition of this book has been used by teachers to analyse and explain the rationale for actions which have become natural and intuitive to them through successful practice.

We realise that any authors who write about the management of children face difficulties, because they are not present in schools and classrooms where the significant events that affect management take place. We hope that we have reduced these difficulties facing us as far as it is possible to reduce them. We are experienced teachers, we are in contact with practising teachers, and we base many descriptive passages on observations in classrooms.

In our experience, it seems that effective teachers develop their own personal management practices without undue concern about the theories that underpin them. What we have tried to do here is to describe effective practice and also explain the theories that support it.

In some ways, effective classroom management is not unlike chess, although the comparison is not altogether satisfactory, because we do not regard teachers and the children in their classes as opponents. But it is true that experienced teachers know about opening moves and their effects on subsequent moves; they know which gambits are risky and they know how to avoid checkmate and how to checkmate others. They also learn to study and respect the other person at the board. But even comprehensive knowledge of openings, middle and end games does not, of itself, ensure success. The knowledge has to be applied with sensitivity and imagination that can only come through practice. At the same time, this practice is improved by reading the accounts and confessions of successful chess players. Classroom practice is improved by studying what others do successfully and understanding the principles on which their practice is based.

We have written about management rather than control in classrooms, because we believe that management emphasises that learning and teaching are complementary activities. Just as successful managers in commerce and industry avoid disputes which disrupt production, so in the classroom successful teachers do not constantly have to demonstrate 'who is the boss'. There are times when teachers must exert their authority clearly and unmistakably, and we do not pretend that it can be otherwise. But we also believe that good classroom management depends more upon teachers and children working equitably together because they are confident together, than upon peremptory instruction and resigned obedience.

Though the fundamentals of classroom management do not change, this new edition has been rearranged into four sections to draw attention to the importance of seeing effective classroom management, not as a simple attribute which individual teachers either have or have not got, but as the product of a combination of skills, knowledge and understanding, which can be fostered by individuals and institutions. Each section refers mnemonically to an aspect of teaching beginning with the letter 'M'.

Management refers to skill in the organisation and presentation of lessons in such a way that all pupils are actively engaged in learning. This requires an ability to analyse the different elements and phases of a lesson, to select and deliver appropriate material and to reduce sources of friction. These issues are discussed in Chapters 1–3.

Mediation refers to knowledge of how to provide the more intensive individual counselling and guidance which some pupils require, how to enhance self-concepts and avoid damaging confrontation in the classroom. This is examined in Chapters 4–7.

Modification refers to understanding the ways in which learning theory can be applied to devising programmes for shaping and changing behaviour through thinking up suitable rewards and punishment. These issues are discussed in Chapter 8.

Monitoring refers to checking the effectiveness of school policies on discipline and pastoral care and how senior management can help colleagues avoid stress and cope with problems in classroom management. These issues are discussed in Chapters 9 and 10.

Though it is possible to see a progression from simple to more complex problems or from responsibilities of the individual to institutional responsibilities, the different perspectives described by the 'four Ms' inevitably overlap and interlock. As with so many aspects of education, effective classroom management depends on the quality of support and guidance within the school as well as the talent of the individual teacher.

Part I

Management

Chapter 1

Four rules of classroom management

Is there some special personal magic which enables some teachers to quieten excitement merely by arriving at the scene, quell misbehaviour with a glance, make classrooms bustle with activity and hum with cheerful industry? Perhaps at this highest level of perfection there may indeed be some extra ingredient of individual charisma but studies of teacher behaviour (Rutter *et al.*, 1979; Wragg, 1984) have noted specific skills which are demonstrated by effective teachers. These skills can be learned and applied by newcomers to the profession.

As McManus (1989) sensibly points out 'teaching is more than the sum of its parts' but it is possible from research, observation and autobiographical anecdote to discern 'four rules' of classroom management applied by successful teachers which like the 'four rules' in arithmetic, once assimilated, can be applied in many different situations.

RULE ONE: GET THEM IN

This rule emphasises the point that a lesson which makes a brisk start will avoid the difficulties which can arise if pupils are not promptly engaged in useful activity. If teachers are pre-occupied with setting up displays, distributing materials or searching for equipment then there are ample opportunities for idling, chatter and other unproductive activities. The activities are of no great disruptive impact in themselves, but they often build up to a cumulative disorder, which leads in turn to further distraction in the form of exhortation, reprimand or even disciplinary action by the teacher which extends the delay in beginning the lesson. The process of 'getting them in' can be seen to involve three phases: greeting, seating and starting.

Greeting

Simply by being there before the class arrives the teacher establishes the role of host receiving the class and he is quietly able to underline his authority by deciding when pupils are invited to enter the room. There is also the vital practical advantage of being able to check that the room is tidy, that materials are available, displays arranged, and necessary instructions or examples are written on the board. This will all help to provide the mental composure essential to relaxed assurance. In larger schools, this tactic may not be easy, though professional commitment appears to be a more significant factor than distance between teaching areas in ensuring a prompt start to lessons (Rutter *et al.*, 1979).

Seating

Although arrangements will vary according to the type of lesson, age of pupils and nature of activity, it is important that initially teachers decide where children should sit. Like entrance to the room, this is another aspect of the natural establishment of responsibility. Teachers may choose to encourage children to sit with friends to promote co-operation or they may deliberately and arbitrarily disperse such centres of potential distraction: but they establish that placement and movement in the classroom are matters which they control. A seating plan showing who sits where quickly enables teachers to learn and use individual names, so although later regrouping will be desirable, it is very useful for at least the first few lessons if a fixed pattern is set and maintained.

Starting

Starting a lesson smoothly and promptly depends not only on managing the physical entrance and disposition of the student body but also the mental tuning-in of the student mind. One teacher interviewed as part of the Teacher Education Project study of first encounters between teachers and new groups of pupils, expertly and neatly sums up how to start a lesson:

> Right at the start of the lesson there is something for them to do: games, workcards, anything, because they rarely arrive at the

same time. I try to create an atmosphere in which they start
science as soon as they come through the door.

(Wragg, 1984)

Whatever the subject or topic each lesson should start with some
activity which occupies every child quietly, whilst teachers deal
with registration, latecomers, lost or malfunctioning equipment.
The type of activity will depend on the age and ability of the child
and the nature of the lesson, but it must be something within each
child's capacity to accomplish without additional help. It should
reinforce previously acquired skills, recap earlier work or set the
scene for new learning. This warming-up period might only last
four or five minutes, perhaps a few sums or a short paragraph to
be read with two or three questions to be answered will be
sufficient to set the tone and establish a calm and positive
atmosphere before moving on to the main content of the lesson.

RULE TWO: GET THEM OUT

Though most disciplinary problems arise from a poor start to a
lesson, the next most vulnerable time providing many opportunities for trouble making is the end of a teaching session. For this
reason 'get them out' is cited as the second rule of classroom
management. Carefully planning the end of each lesson is a crucial
part of the way in which experienced teachers successfully handle
transition from one activity to another. As Gray and Richer (1988)
put it, 'structure at the end of a lesson is all too easily lost in a sigh
of relief that it is nearly over'. The lasting effect of an interesting
learning experience can be wasted and pleasantly developing
relationships between teacher and class can be spoilt if a
productive session dissolves into a noisy, chaotic and stressful
finale. So teachers need to consider the two phases of concluding
a lesson and dismissing a class.

Concluding

An orderly procedure for stopping work should include
consolidation and reinforcement of learning and this is difficult to
achieve if children are still busy writing or engaged in collecting
books and gathering materials together. It is helpful to give an
early warning that it will be time to stop in 'two minutes precisely'
or whatever is a suitable time to avoid stopping pupils in

mid-sentence. It is vital that all work must cease in good time for material to be collected, books put away and still give opportunity for some revision and recapitulation. This could take the form of a brief question and answer session which will enable the teacher to check on how successfully objectives have been attained or identify points which require further attention. Additionally or sometimes alternatively this time should be used for a summary reminding the class of what has been covered during the lesson and how this links in to previous learning or prepares the way for the next activity.

Gray and Richer (1988) point out how valuable it is to use this time to give positive feedback to pupils, praising good work and reassuring those who have had difficulties that next time things will be different. It is an opportunity to refresh, restate and reinforce the theme of the lesson. It can also be a good idea to reserve some time for a game, quiz or story so that the conclusion of the lesson becomes a reward for earlier effort, particularly for those who may find the main subject content a bit of a struggle. Ending on a light and positive note in this way should leave even the least competent pupils feeling that though it will never be a favoured activity, even a difficult subject offers them some possibility of pleasure and enjoyment.

Dismissing

Decisions about the precise method for dismissing a class will vary according to the age of the pupils. As Gray and Richer (1988) suggest, 'Arms folded, sitting up straight!' or similar ritualised instructions may be appropriate for controlling young children, but they are more likely to provoke confrontation with older pupils. Yet some sequence or pattern which facilitates the movement of bodies from inside to outside the classroom with minimum contact with furniture, equipment or each other does need to be established. Otherwise the teacher will finish up wasting valuable preparation time clearing debris from the floor, readjusting desks and tables or remonstrating with pupils who ought already to be somewhere else.

It is important to remember that classes are never just leaving one place; they are going to another. Children should be helped to cue in to their next activity. Consider the following vignette, its origin is American but its truth is universal.

Teacher: It's time for PE now, everybody get ready. Table 1, line up at the door. Don't forget to pass your papers in. OK Table 2, go ahead. Put your counting sticks away, everyone. Billy be quiet. Why aren't you cleaning up?

Students: Ms Jones we need our coats; it's cold out.

Teacher: For goodness sake, everybody sit down. You are much too noisy.

(Lemlech, 1979)

Here, because the teacher has not thought out the sequence for concluding the lesson and dismissing the class, the pupils have become confused and a quite unnecessary conflict has arisen over their behaviour. Some simple system of traffic regulation has to be established in early meetings with a class. Eventually, self-discipline based on awareness of the teacher's reasonable expectations of polite behaviour may suffice to ensure an orderly departure, but initially some standard routine for dismissal one table or one section at a time is likely to be necessary. The sequence should be clearing up and collecting books and material, checking up on learning and giving feedback, enjoying a game or other relaxing end to the session, setting up the group for its next move (in the example above, arranging for the children to collect their coats) and finally supervising departure, if necessary standing at the door to continue supervision of progress down the corridor.

RULE THREE: GET ON WITH IT

In this context 'it' refers to the main part of the lesson, the nature of its content and the manner of its presentation. Pupils' feelings of self-esteem and sense of competence in a particular subject area will depend to a considerable extent on the teacher's ability to 'get on with it'.

Content

Difficulties in learning and consequent problems with behaviour often happen because the content of a lesson is not matched to the ability of the pupils to whom it is delivered. Because persistent failure can easily result in disgruntled disaffection, careful scrutiny of the curriculum by subject departments and by individual teachers is needed to ensure that it is appropriate. Methods and materials should also be closely examined to see that learning experiences are suitable and study tasks are attainable for pupils with a range and diversity of aptitudes and abilities. Raban and Postlethwaite (1988) offer some useful advice on how this can be done by finding out what pupils already know, starting a little further back to build on what is understood, planning small steps towards each teaching goal and being prepared to adjust these plans if progress is not being made.

Within an individual lesson, variety and pace are needed to maintain momentum. Activities planned for the beginning and conclusion of the session will go some way to achieving these aims, but it is also important to provide variety in the main body of the lesson particularly in double periods. Breaking topics up into smaller units, switching between quiet individual study and arranging some active, co-operative learning in pairs or groups will go some way to combating the inexorable law that the alertness of the brain is inversely proportionate to the numbness of the posterior!

Though difficult to attain, the ambition to see that every child has something finished and something marked in every lesson will help maintain the pace of teaching. Such immediate feedback and reinforcement is especially important for pupils with learning difficulties, whose previous failures leave them needing frequent reassurance that they are on the right track. These children will also benefit from teachers taking particular care to deliver instructions clearly and precisely since 'if children know what we want them to do, they will usually do it' (Lovitt, 1977).

The momentum or flow of classroom activity is vital to discipline because interruptions lead to distraction and loss of interest for pupils and teachers. Although a general briskness sets the normally appropriate tone, there are also occasions when teaching less and allowing more time for practice or discussion are necessary. Finding the correct balance is not always easy, too much of the same thing becomes tedious, too many changes become confusing, but most lessons should involve some listening, some looking, some thinking, some talking, some reading and some writing.

Manner

Positive relationships develop from the manner in which people communicate with each other. For teachers, this means thinking about how they address and question children and how they convey expectations about behaviour. The atmosphere in a classroom is like any 'weather system' subject to change and the effective teacher is skilled at spotting and dispersing a minor disturbance before it builds up into a major depression. As in meteorology, successful forecasting requires alertness to early warning signals and these are most readily picked up by teachers who display what Kounin (1970) and Brophy and Evertson (1976) have described respectively as 'withitness' and 'smoothness'.

'Withitness' is the somewhat dated term which describes the timeless virtue of being able to provide work at a suitable level and administer a system in which pupils know what to do, where to get help if needed and what to do next when they have finished an assignment. For example, where there are difficulties in reading or comprehension, help can be provided through topic guidelines, summaries and key word charts giving explanations and spellings.

'Smoothness' refers to the ease with which pupils move from one activity to another. Transitions can be handled more easily and problems avoided by ensuring that supplementary activities are readily available to usefully occupy anyone who has completed their original assignment. This enables the teacher to ensure that all the class will be ready to change together from one activity or location to another. The smooth flow of classroom life is also helped by teachers avoiding too many disciplinary interruptions. The more that punishments are dealt out, the more nagging that goes on, the more negative comments that are made, the more tension will increase and the more the class will be distracted from the work in hand.

The manner in which a teacher addresses a class reflects an attitude and conveys a message not only through what is said but also through how it is said. Before speaking to the class it is essential that attention is gained by getting pupils to stop work and listen carefully. It follows that any information to be delivered in this way should be vital enough to merit the inevitable interruption to the lesson. Facial expression and tone of voice are as important to any communication as making sure that it is being heard. A persistent frown or intimidating scowl is likely to convey anxiety as much as displeasure and an angry shout can awkwardly modulate into a shriek more suggestive of hysteria than confident control.

The old adage 'quiet teacher, quiet class' offers good advice but should be followed with some caution as the comment 'inaudible teacher, insufferable class' may equally be true. A clear and sufficient volume is required to satisfy an assumption, that in any class there is likely to be at least one child with some hearing loss, but speech should be delivered as Fontana (1986) advises in 'a voice which children find it pleasant to listen to, and a voice which the teacher can use all day without undue strain.'

The importance of teachers using their eyes to communicate is emphasised by what might be described as a 'lighthouse technique' for addressing the class recommended by Marland (1975). Each sentence is spoken to an individual child with established eye contact. At the end of a sentence or as a new idea is introduced or as the theme changes the teacher's gaze is shifted and eye contact established with another pupil in another part of the room to whom the next comment is expressed. A third pupil is chosen as the focus for the next comment and so on. In this way the teacher's eye sweeps the room like the beam from a lighthouse and the teacher's brain picks up a 'feel' for what is going on in different areas of the room. Thus is the impression of 'eyes in the back of my head' fostered particularly if teachers noticing some minor misbehaviour in one part of the room, wait until they have turned to address someone elsewhere before naming the wrongdoers and requiring them to cease their transgression.

Another aspect of the manner of teaching is the point and purpose of the teacher's use of questions. Are they seen as tricks and traps set to catch the unwary and inattentive? If so, they become a likely source of negative interaction serving to keep attention focused, but at a cost of potential embarrassment and humiliation for the less able pupil. A more positive orientation is for teachers to see questioning as a means of checking whether material is understood and to treat an incorrect answer as the teacher's fault for inadequate explanation and an occasion for further expansion and illustration instead of reprimand. Of course, this may not always be true, but it offers a perspective in which questions are a source of feedback rather than friction with answers responded to with praise if possible, with tact if not.

RULE FOUR: GET ON WITH THEM

Teachers develop good personal relationships with their pupils by fostering mutual trust and respect. To do this effectively teachers need to be aware of each child as an individual and be sensitive to the mood of the class as a whole. This means knowing who's who and keeping track of what's going on.

Who's who?

Awareness of individual differences begins with the mundane but essential task of learning names and putting them accurately to faces. Once a child's name is known, discipline is immediately easier because wrongdoers will realise that they can be identified and because requests or rebukes can be personalised. Direct instructions to 'be quiet please Quentin', or 'sit up straight Cydonia' are much more likely to be heeded than vaguely addressed summonses to 'that boy at the back' or 'the girl over there'. However recognition has a much more positive aspect too since it conveys the teacher's interest and reflects a willingness to spend time and effort in learning names.

Keeping the same seating plan, at least for the first few meetings with a group enables the teacher to use names correctly albeit at first by discreet reference to the plan. An active strategy should then be employed to revisualise the plan, to scan the room mentally recalling names whilst pupils are working and to always address questions and comments by name. Attempting to fill in a blank copy of the plan when the pupils are not present can be very revealing about a teachers own perception of individual characters. Whilst the bright, the backward and the baleful may come readily to mind it is often less easy to remember pupils who are less demanding of attention, though they may need it just as much.

Other useful tactics in fixing names and faces are adding a brief written comment using the pupil's name each time work is marked and taking every opportunity to chat informally to children outside class in playground, corridor and dining room so that some additional background information is added to the teacher's mental picture. At first most information will be social, perhaps which football team or pop group is supported, but together with the academic information gleaned from observation in class a fuller rounder picture of each individual will emerge. For such tactics to be successful it is essential that they are based on a natural and genuine personal interest not merely an assumed and intrusive nosiness.

What's going on?

Few classes or groups of pupils within a class are likely to be so purposefully malevolent as to set out on a planned campaign of disruption. However, individually minor irritations can develop collectively into more serious sources of friction. As suggested by the analogy with weather forecasting mentioned earlier, alertness to early warning signs can enable accurate prediction of developing storms but unlike meteorologists teachers can do something about it. Acquiring this sensitivity to the class atmosphere depends on a combination of mobility and marking.

Mobility involves the avoidance of teachers becoming 'desk-bound' by queues of children waiting for attention or by over-reliance on a lecturing style of teaching. Moving around the room, quietly marking work in progress, offering advice and guidance keeps attention on the task in hand. It is a natural contact between teacher and pupil which provides immediate feedback and means that if attention has wandered the teacher's response can be to offer help with an assumed difficulty rather than reprimand about misbehaviour.

When working at one pupil's desk or with a group around a table, a brief glance around the rest of the room will identify any potential trouble spots. Often merely moving to an area where shuffling feet or an increasing volume of noise may indicate the beginnings of disruption can refocus attention but if not, then a mild rebuke, quietly spoken to an individual can be more effective and certainly less distracting than a loud public admonition.

Through this active involvement at child level, allied to the aforementioned 'lighthouse' technique when addressing the class as a whole, the teacher becomes more responsive to the prevailing mood of the group and better able to judge the times for emphasis on serious brisk endeavour or for more relaxed and light-hearted amusement.

FRAMEWORK FOR ANALYSIS

Following the four rules outlined above will not in itself provide a panacea for trouble-free teaching, but it does suggest a framework for analysing aspects of lesson planning and management which contribute to a productive partnership in learning between teachers and pupils. By attending to the different phases of their lesson and reflecting on personal relationships with pupils, teachers can begin to identify areas where a changed approach might be needed. Two important areas in which further analysis will be helpful are classroom organisation and reducing sources of friction.

Chapter 2

Analysing classroom organisation

This area can itself be considered in terms of a framework consisting of three related aspects of teaching:

I The *milieu* or classroom environment within which relationships develop.
II The *methods* by which teaching is delivered.
III The *materials* through which learning is experienced.

I THE MILIEU

If the four 'goals of misbehaviour' described by Dreikurs, Grunwald and Pepper (1971) are examined, it appears that problems arise far more often from the first two of these, warding off inadequacy and gaining attention, than from the more threatening goals of seeking power or revenge. Certainly the latter often play some part in serious conflict and confrontation. This chapter, however, focuses on how analysis of different aspects of classroom organisation can reduce the potential for more serious disruption by ensuring that children do not become discouraged by feelings of inadequacy and incompetence or seek attention in anti-social ways because they have lost interest in a subject and lack confidence in their ability to cope with it.

In this context, Weber (1982) describes two very relevant concepts of 'encouragement' and 'momentum' which are essential to engaging and maintaining pupils' interest and motivation. He defines 'encouragement' as 'an affirmation of belief in the pupil's potential and capacity to do better'. It is this approach which stops teachers becoming defeatist or classes demoralised when difficulties in learning are encountered. It is demonstrated by the manner in which enthusiasm permeates the teacher's planning and presentation, combining the ability to transmit a personal fascination with the subject being taught and a genuine enjoyment of the company of the students to whom it is being taught.

Weber defines 'momentum' as the intrinsic phenomenon which keeps learners moving forward even when difficulties are encountered. It involves a realisation of an ability to cope and a capacity for achievement in a subject. It is promoted by the teacher's skill in ensuring that even less able pupils have sufficient experience of success to generate self-motivation.

By examining their classroom organisation teachers can identify ways of avoiding pupil misbehaviour which develops as a means of warding off inadequacy and identify ways of improving encouragement and momentum. The following framework for analysis is not intended to provide a revelatory insight, it is simply a reminder of those aspects of lesson planning which contribute most to the development of a smooth and effective partnership in learning between teachers and pupils. This analysis of classroom organisation involves consideration of milieu, methods and materials.

There is a social climate or atmosphere which sets the prevailing mood in every classroom. Children do bring anxieties and antagonisms from home, playground and other lessons, but it is the teacher's approach which mainly determines the state of the classroom environment. Successful innovations with methods and materials may crucially depend on the nature of the milieu into which they are introduced. Establishing an atmosphere which is favourable to change, because pupils and teachers are confident together, requires the development of good relationships based on positive expectations.

RELATIONSHIPS

Teachers' expectations are conveyed to pupils in a variety of subtle ways which have a powerful influence in helping or hindering the development of the pupil's self-image as a competent or incompetent learner. Differential expectations are shown by the way teachers talk to different individuals or groups, by the way they question them, by the type of tasks set for them and by the amount of time spent with them.

In a celebrated experiment, Rosenthal and Jacobson (1968)

demonstrated the power of high expectation. Teachers were told that the performance of certain pupils on a new psychological test showed that they were about to experience a period of rapid intellectual growth. Although in fact chosen at random, the identified pupils' performance on tests of general ability and reading achievement at the end of the year was measurably better than the performance of their unselected but equally able classmates. This demonstration has not proved easy to replicate. Perhaps wide and possibly exaggerated publicity for the original study made teachers wary of psychologists bearing gifted children!

Good and Brophy (1980) dismiss as oversimplification the view that elevated expectation in itself produces a self-fulfilling prophecy for success. They advanced a more sophisticated perception that a teacher's knowledge, observation and inferences based on pupil performance, interact with personal feelings and reactions, so that expectations are being constantly shaped and altered by contacts made over tasks and activities in the classroom. Promoting cordial relationships and enhancing positive attitudes will depend to a considerable extent on how such learning experiences are organised.

Differential expectations are inevitable. It is neither possible nor desirable to expect the same level of performance from all pupils as they all have different abilities and different individual needs, but teachers should be aware of how their behaviour may be interpreted. Brophy and Good (1974) give examples of how teachers they observed behaved differently towards pupils of whom they have high or low expectations.

Over-reactive teachers had rigid and stereotyped perceptions, dismissing the 'slow learner's' capacity to improve or the 'troublemaker's' potential for reform. They tended to underestimate what less able children could do and they were inclined to give up easily with them. These teachers spent much more of their time with high achievers who were encouraged to dominate class discussion.

Reactive teachers were less likely to be inflexible or negative in their approach, but were passive in their acceptance of low achievement rather than active in trying to compensate for differences in ability. Through neglect rather than rejection, less able pupils received less attention than brighter pupils.

Proactive teachers were readier to take the initiative in overcoming problems with learning, making realistic judgements in planning individual instruction and engaging low as well as high achievers in balanced participation in discussion and other activities.

Some teachers, though striving to be proactive, inadvertently over-compensate and in attempting to accommodate the less able pupil by an overtly sympathetic attitude, they merely emphasise and draw attention to the child's inadequacies. Additional support for individuals should be as unobtrusive as possible and designed to emphasise similarities with other children rather than differences from them. Fulsome praise for patently inadequate work or persistent and publicised setting of evidently easier work can make a pupil feel as if they are being singled out for special embarrassment, as much as being picked out for special treatment.

RULES AND ROUTINES

Other elements in determining the state of the classroom environment are rules and routines. Rules define the boundaries for behaviour within a classroom. They are in effect the formal statement of the teacher's expectations about what pupils may and may not do. As McManus (1989) points out, pupils invariably spend some time discovering and testing teachers' rules. They want to find out how far they can go and 'the less specific and convincing the teacher the more they will explore the boundaries of what they suspect to be permissible'.

It is important therefore to state clearly and precisely, what are the boundaries of the permissible, whilst avoiding the two problems noted by Gray and Richer (1988): once rules are stated the teacher's credibility hinges upon ability to enforce them and infringement of rules is 'the quickest route to confrontation'. It is therefore sensible to reduce the number of formal rules to a minimum and their purpose clearly explained, so that time, effort and authority are not unnecessarily expended on injunction and enforcement.

In advising on school rules the Elton Report (DES, 1989) suggests that 'obscure, arbitrary or petty rules discredit the whole code' and this applies equally to individual classroom rules. Indeed without seeking total conformity to a rigid code, it is vital that there should be a consistent and predictable pattern of teacher response to pupil behaviour. Glynn (1992) makes the point that this is not an easy task as teachers differ widely in their interpretation of what is acceptable behaviour: what may be seen as merely inappropriate behaviour to one teacher may be an intolerable affront to the dignity of another. But as Glynn argues, achieving a staff consensus on responses to pupil behaviour is likely to be a lengthy and protracted business, but it is an essential area of school policy which needs regular review.

Routines regulate the flow of activities within the classroom and they also help reduce the complexities of learning to a more predictable sequence which helps pupils to plan work and anticipate events. Weber (1982) shows how settled patterns of lesson organisation where teachers adopt an agreed approach can help pupils cope with the complexities of a secondary school timetable. An example of a routine similar to that applied by Weber and his colleagues would be an agreement that all lessons should:

- Start with seatwork, recapping material previously taught.
- Introduce new learning by talk or demonstration.
- Make sure that new ideas are understood by questioning.
- Practice examples with group and individuals.
- Look back by reviewing new learning and linking it to old.
- Enjoy a game, story or other relaxation.

This plan provides the mnemonic acronym SIMPLE, itself a reminder that such routines should not become overelaborate as they mark out distinct phases or stages which pace the rhythm of the lesson and ease the transition from one activity to another. Gray and Richer (1988) offer the valuable perception that there are always two aspects to any classroom agenda. Well-planned routines establish a balance between the work agenda and the social agenda ensuring that teaching takes place with a clear purpose in a congenial atmosphere. Maintaining that balance also requires careful consideration of methods and materials.

II THE METHODS

In some schools the conditions and consequences of learning appear to be arranged in ways which might be expected to discourage all but the brightest, most competent and self-motivated pupils. Indeed Booth and Coulby (1987) suggest that attitudes fostered by certain approaches to the curriculum may actually produce pupil disaffection. Either overtly or covertly decisions about streaming, setting and admission to prestigious examination courses sometimes send a message that a pupil is not valued by the school. Having received such a message pupils may respond with reciprocal antagonism. As one boy explained to Hargreaves (1967), one of his friends, by this time a leading member of the C stream group labelled as delinquent and disruptive, had started school life in the A stream but changed his character as he was 'demoted'. As Hargreaves' informant memorably put it, he would have been 'all right', if only the teachers had 'kept him clever'.

Curricular considerations

Do schools do enough to see that sufficient support is given to avoid this wasteful process of educational and social detachment? An emphasis on academic achievement is a positive feature of a school's ethos, but if it becomes the only source of success and esteem within the school, then it can lead to problems for many pupils. Smith (1990; 1992a; 1992b) discusses ways in which curriculum development policy and support teaching can help pupils with learning, emotional and behavioural difficulties in mainstream schools; but it is not just pupils with clearly identified and 'statemented' special educational needs whom schools should seek to 'keep clever'. Pupils not achieving their potential will include not only underachievers, low attainers or slow learners but also otherwise bright pupils, who may have specific learning difficulties in particular areas of the curriculum or may be disadvantaged by a school's inability to adapt to individuals from a diversity of social and cultural backgrounds. With this in mind, the Elton Report (DES, 1989) urged schools to examine carefully their policies for setting, banding or streaming in order to avoid feelings of rejection and hostility.

However, even as these thoughts were being gathered by the Committee of Enquiry, they were being overtaken, perhaps overwhelmed, by the tidal wave of changes consequent upon the 1988 Education Act and its attendant philosophy that 'money will follow the pupil', likely to encourage a competitive approach based on schools promoting an image of academic excellence demonstrated by examination success. Such changes may well pressure schools towards adopting methods which will separate and segregate rather than incorporate the disaffected. With competition between schools, devoting time and resources to pupils with problems could be seen as less productive than a similar investment in raising levels of performance at the upper end of the ability spectrum.

None the less it is likely that most schools will continue to organise classes of mixed ability and even in the most selective system there will always be children of comparatively less competence in any given subject area. So teaching methods must still be sufficiently flexible to cope with a range of capacities for learning. This requires making decisions about teaching methods which imply different arrangements for class, group and individual teaching and consequent consideration of classroom layout and design.

Working with groups

The traditional presentation of knowledge and information is most readily accomplished through the traditional arrangement of desks or tables in serried ranks facing the teacher. Wheldall and Merrett (1992) have demonstrated that seating children in rows rather than around tables increases on-task behaviour. It should be noted that Wheldall and Merrett emphasise the point that their research should not be taken as advocating this arrangement for all work, but that 'teachers should vary seating arrangements to suit the task in hand'.

Where group work is undertaken this can be used for assigning different tasks to groups organised according to levels of ability. If such groups become permanent across a wide range of classroom activities, there is a danger that this approach will lead to stigmatisation and the lowering of teacher expectation and pupil aspiration. Used sparingly for specific purposes and regularly reviewed and revised, ability grouping for part of a lesson can undoubtedly help match tasks more closely to stages of development. One benefit of the National Curriculum ought to be the manner in which awareness of performance on attainment targets should draw attention to the different stages of development within a class of children of a similar age.

Primary schools have long been aware of this challenge and secondary schools have become increasingly sensitive to individual differences, particularly in relation to providing support for pupils with learning difficulties in mainstream classes.

However, even within schools firmly committed to the concept of mixed-ability teaching, what happens in practice might more accurately be described as 'mid-ability' teaching. Anxious to retain control and cohesion over groups with a diversity of abilities and aptitudes, teachers tend to pitch lessons at a level at which most of their pupils will be able to perform adequately. Frequently this will leave the more able unstretched and the less able untouched by the experience.

Kerry and Sands' (1984) research showed that in the comprehensive schools which they studied, whole-class teaching predominated and where group work did take place it was limited to small sections of the class all undertaking the same undifferentiated whole-class tasks. There were few examples of what Kerry and Sands describe as 'educational group work' with pupils engaged in different tasks requiring co-operation and pooling of resources. Managing such group work is not an easy organisational option, it requires high quality teaching skills to motivate and supervise learning in this situation. It is well worth the effort, however, because work in smaller groups offers opportunities for increasing pupil visibility, encouraging communication and stimulating competitive learning without undermining individual self-confidence.

In the traditional layout of desks in rows for whole-class teaching or lecturing, the teacher's attention tends to focus on a limited 'action zone' in the front and middle rows (Good and Brophy, 1984). This limits the visibility of certain pupils outside the central area and may incidentally explain why teachers, when themselves on training courses, instinctively fill up lecture theatres from the rear and periphery!

Whilst the bright, the backward and the baleful will always make their presence felt wherever they sit, it is all too easy for more modest pupils to fade into anonymity in large classes taught in the traditional manner. Working in smaller groups, the strengths and weaknesses of all individuals become more evident because they are more clearly visible to teachers reacting to a series of 'action zones'.

Small groups encourage communication because it is easier to talk when directly face to face with someone rather than addressing the backs of heads or coping with the embarrassment of everyone turning around to look at a possibly nervous and inarticulate speaker. Thus, whether contributing to an academic problem-solving task or in more general socialising, the less confident pupil is given greater opportunities to participate and develop interpersonal skills.

Group work is considered usually in terms of co-operative learning, but it also offers possibilities for competitive learning in a less threatening setting than individual performance. Astute tailoring of tasks or questions can ensure that group or team success depends as much on the least able as on the most able member. Competition can be an enjoyable method of enlivening the learning and recall of essential facts, but it carries the threat of being the source of heightened illumination of individual ignorance. Working with groups offers the chance of providing the element of excitement without the potential limelight hogging or ego bruising of individual competition.

Classroom layout

If teachers do wish to work with small groups, then thought needs to be given to the arrangement of classroom furniture and which design and layout is best suited to the intended task. Often group work means pupils sitting round tables or desks put together to form a similar base. Waterhouse (1983) likens the random arrangement of such groups to a 'dining room' approach with the teacher and resources located at the front of the room as a sort of academic serving hatch. The successful ordering of this arrangement, as anyone who has ever done 'dinner duty' will confirm, depends on careful regulation of visits to the servery. Whilst it is easy enough to control the allotment of second helpings or delay delivery of desserts until everyone has finished the main course, demands for academic service are less predictable and almost inevitably queues of the eager or overdependent build up diverting the teacher's attention or masking the teacher's observation of the rest of the class.

This arrangement also means that for a large part of every lesson many children sit with their backs to the teacher. This makes it difficult for teachers to make sure children are attending and if everyone is asked to turn round and face the teacher, there is a shifting of chairs and jostling of bodies which inevitably distracts and breaks the momentum and continuity of the lesson. Negotiating the route to and from the teacher's desk, whether in search of guidance or materials, adds another source for contact, comment and confusion.

Waterhouse (1983) suggests that most of these problems can be overcome by adopting a 'peripheral' system. This involves placing desks or tables around the edges of the room with the teacher's desk located in the centre of the room, together with 'resource islands' from which children draw, as necessary, supplies of stationery and other materials and where they consult reference books or find new workcards. This should make traffic regulation more manageable and also make it easier to focus attention on the teacher, when information and instructions need to be given.

Lemlech (1988) suggests using 'learning centres', described as 'an environment arranged to accomplish a particular instructional purpose'. This is a similar idea to 'resource islands' but with materials grouped by theme instead of function. Learning centres are parts of the classroom, where tables, desks and bookshelves are organised with books, paper, art or writing materials gathered together for activities selected to extend and enrich understanding of a particular curricular topic, or to give extra practice and reinforcement in using a specific skill. These centres might be arranged by subject area: language, maths, science; or they might each relate to an aspect of a skill: reading comprehension, listening with understanding, writing and spelling. The classroom might also be designed to accommodate 'interest centres' for student activity and choice during free time.

Cangelosi (1988) discusses the attributes of an 'ideal classroom' and suggests that the room should be adaptable for whole class lectures, small group tasks and individual study laid out in such a way that the teacher has a good vantage point for supervision, easy access to move quickly and easily to any pupil and adequate storage for materials and equipment. Cangelosi then provides an illustrated tale of how one teacher attains this ideal, changing the furniture and design of a traditional high school 'obstacle course' of a classroom, through a series of adaptations involving volunteer labour, parental support and gifts of 'surplus' furniture into a flexible working environment with its own mini-library and quiet room.

Providing support

Successful group work and differentiation of the curriculum for pupils with a diversity of learning abilities and styles depends on establishing a system for gaining access to support and guidance when needed. Otherwise teachers attempting to work with small groups or individuals may find their good intentions frustrated by constant distracting 'low order' requests for help with spelling or advice on what to do next once the initial task is finished (Bennett *et al.*, 1984). These problems can be alleviated if careful thought is given to the allocation of tasks and making the best use of any available human resources.

The amount and difficulty of work from groups and individuals can be regulated by allocation based on one of three systems which can be described as rota, quota or branching. A rota will, as its name suggests, rotate groups through different activities with set periods of time at different learning centres or tackling different tasks. The time given might be a short session during one lesson or spread over different lessons. This system can ensure that not all pupils are seeking the same information at the same time and that the teacher is able to introduce and demonstrate new material to one group while others are engaged in activity-practising and applying knowledge and skills already acquired.

The quota system simply extends the rota by fixing a quota of assignments to be completed by an individual or group within a period of time. This leaves more discretion to the pupil about when any given activity should be undertaken, but provides a range of options if access to certain materials or the teacher's attention has to be delayed because they are already engaged by others. This system requires careful judgement about appropriate levels and amounts of work to be set and good simple record keeping so that teacher and pupil can easily tell what has been done and what remains to be done.

Branching offers firmer retention of control for the teacher with all the class starting together on an activity, listening to a lecture, story or video presentation and then 'branching' into different follow-up work. Some who have quickly grasped the new ideas may move on to more testing work, others may need more practice at the same level, others may need further explanation or simpler examples. Another application might be class work for part of the lesson followed by dispersion to learning or interest centres for the rest of the time.

Whichever system is selected, it will be helped by the preparation of clear topic outlines or study guides, which can be consulted before teachers need to be asked for further explanation. These guides should include keywords and definitions of key concepts as well as clear instruction on the stages and sequence of the activity. Waterhouse (1983) gives additional advice on how teachers can develop study units, organise the 'rotating circus' through which groups 'tour' areas of study and ensure that there is sufficient supplementary material to occupy 'waiting time' between moving from one activity to another.

Support from other adults can ease many of the organisational problems posed by flexible working with class, group and individual teaching. However sheer weight of adult numbers is not in itself sufficient to ensure that effective support is provided, whether by other teachers, classroom ancillaries or parent helpers. Even when fellow professionals of equal status work together, Ferguson and Adams (1982) indicate some of the problems which can arise. In their observation of remedial teachers working alongside mainstream colleagues, they note that although ostensibly there to provide expert help, the remedial specialists were in practice perceived and treated by teachers and their pupils as 'teacher's aides', 'helpful visitors' and 'faithful retainers'. This hardly promotes the idea of co-operative and collaborative team teaching which is at the heart of recent changes in thinking about providing support for pupils with special educational needs.

If even fellow teachers are reduced to a subordinate role in this way, it is not surprising that other adults may only be accorded a minor role, which does not encourage children to look to them for help. Writing initially in the context of research on team teaching in special schools for children with severe learning difficulties but more recently extending the concept to mainstream support, Thomas (1988) suggests a more effective approach to room management. He claims that there is more active engagement in learning, if teachers and others in the team decide on specific interchangeable roles, so that instead of minding a particular child, group or area of the room, each adult takes responsibility for certain aspects of work. The 'individual helper' will teach 'one-to-one', the 'activity manager' will supervise groups and the 'mover' will organise the distribution of materials, arrangement of furniture and take care of any interruptions such as the delivery of messages.

The crucial point about this approach is that it assigns precise duties and clear responsibilities, so that everyone knows what they should be doing and pupils understand to whom they should turn for what sort of help. This exact definition is even more important where other pupils are used as 'peer tutors'. Unless carefully planned additional help in the classroom may merely add to confusion and distraction and as with any method, success will also depend on the selection and presentation of suitable material.

III THE MATERIALS

Three questions about work prepared for any lesson are suggested by Braine, Kerry and Pilling (1990).

Is the prepared work:
- relevant to all pupils needs?
- presented in a way which will interest all, providing basic understanding for the weak but a stimulus to stretch the most able?
- sufficient to fill the allocated time?

Responding to these questions involves consideration of choice of subject matter and difficulty of tasks, readability of texts and clarity of instruction and approaches to setting and marking assignments.

Subject matter

To an increasing extent decisions about course content will be determined by the National Curriculum and its attainment targets. However the choice of curriculum material and its presentation and adaptation will remain the responsibility of individual teachers. By addressing pertinent questions, the relevance and suitability of their material and its delivery can be analysed. Questions, such as the following, should be considered. Is a subject area one in which the pupil has previously failed? Is this failure reinforced by the pupil's own awareness of his low achievement? If incompetence has been stressed in the past, certain subjects are approached by children in such a defeatist manner that they are ready to give up before they even start.

It is not enough for teachers to remain doggedly cheerful in the face of ignorance and incomprehension. Though preferable to irritation and scorn, sympathy too can sometimes add to a sense of humiliation. The teacher needs to convey a belief that this time the child really can succeed. This belief should be based on a genuine effort to reorganise, restructure and redesign material so that, although content and skills to be mastered remain the same, the experience of learning them is changed. Just as a failed commercial product is often successfully repackaged and relaunched, so teachers need constantly to resell subject areas. Even if previous failure has produced a thorough dislike of a subject as a whole, a fresh approach can stimulate interest in a particular topic or get children to tackle specific skills with a new vigour. One simple example is the way in which even older slow learners who would baulk at yet another attempt to learn number bonds or multiplication tables will readily tackle the same calculations disguised as algebra equations.

Presentation

Is material presented in a manner which captures the pupil's interest? Do pupils get bored easily? Do they respond better to certain parts of the lesson? Although a predictable pattern to lessons provides 'support from routine', this does not mean that curriculum materials and presentational formats should remain unchanged. The unremitting plod through a standard textbook can be the most dispiriting part of failure in a particular subject. In planning to avoid this, ingenuity is needed to provide a variety of lesson content. Film, television, radio and tape recording can all be useful, and computers are becoming an increasingly familiar teaching aid, offering a particularly attractive method of taking the drudgery out of drill and practice.

Variety can also be achieved by arranging a mixture of oral and written work, individual and group activity. Supplementary worksheets enable teachers to tailor content to the needs of their own pupils, but there is a danger that the spirit duplicator becomes a substitute for spirited teaching and children face what has been described as 'death by a thousand word cards' (Wragg, 1978).

Interest is often easier to gain than to retain. Novel displays or demonstrations, stimulating questions or unusual statements can successfully 'hook' attention. Unless intending to give a lecture (a format only suited to academic work with highly motivated students), the teacher should aim to shift the focus of this attention from himself to some pupil-centred activity. This process will be helped and a purpose will be given to the lesson if this intention is clearly indicated in a brief outline at the start of the lesson, which tells the pupil what the lesson is going to be about and what he will be expected to do.

Difficulty of tasks

Are tasks set at a level of difficulty which offers some measure of challenge, but also a chance of success? Do children get stuck and fail to complete their work? Do some children manage in class, but fail with homework? Martin and Lauridsen (1974) suggest that it sometimes appears as if schools set out to exacerbate failure by moving their less able pupils too rapidly through the curriculum. 'If a student is having trouble with simple addition, move the whole class ahead to fractions and leave him further and further behind'.

Thus tasks need to be set with the individual, rather than the class average, in mind. In the demonstration phase of the lesson, some children will need more time to answer questions or grasp ideas. Careful questioning should alert the teacher to any problems, and these can often be solved by giving further examples or restating an idea in simpler terms. Although it is necessary to beware of overelaboration slowing down the progress of the rest of the class, the greater danger is that somebody will 'get two, three steps behind and then it's too late' (Weber, 1982).

During the practice phase, difficulties show up when children who clearly understand the instructions nevertheless get stuck. This may be a symptom of a problem which needs deeper diagnosis, but in the first instance emphasis should be placed on helping strugglers to keep up. Sometimes this can be achieved by giving an extra clue or prompting a correct answer by narrowing a field of search: 'It's near London on the map' or 'Look at the second paragraph'. On other occasions, it is more appropriate to modify the assignment, cutting down the required amount of work or sidestepping the difficult problem for the time being. 'Just do the first ten' or 'Leave that question, go on to the next one'. For certain children work will need to be broken down into shorter segments with more frequent feedback, for example, marking every five sums instead of every twenty.

The technique for group teaching described earlier as

'branching' is a very useful means of ensuring that work demands are related to a pupil's potential and capacity to respond. Grouping will also ease the arrangement of extra coaching or repetition of examples, without delaying the rest of the class.

If difficulties are encountered because children do not have the prerequisite skills, then arrangements need to be made for revision or reteaching of those skills. Often teachers assume that children have certain skills because these have been taught in previous years, but, although taught, the skills may not have been learnt or mastered. In the meantime, alternative easier work can be provided, while taking account of the problem by setting a more attainable target for the next session. It is useless, for example, to attempt long division if the short version has not been mastered.

Some children will be able to work competently enough, but only at a pace that leaves them adrift of their classmates. This may be due to distraction, through chatting with friends or being too interested in other people's work, instead of getting on with their own. In extreme cases, this may necessitate moving children away from the source of distraction. Usually a reminder of the need for concentration on the task in hand will suffice, particularly if the prohibition on discussion is only for a limited period. 'You may talk to your neighbour when you've both finished this exercise'.

It is important to ensure that work is completed as homework, if not within the lesson. However, this should not become too hefty an imposition on children who are working steadily, if rather slowly. In exceptional circumstances, losses may need to be cut by the abandonment of a particularly difficult exercise and its replacement by something easier. This should rarely happen once a teacher has had an opportunity to assess his pupils' abilities.

Homework should be set to reinforce learning that has taken place in school. It should provide further practice, rather than introduce new ideas. Children who might be able to manage with the assistance of the teacher can easily become confused when expected to cope with variations and 'surprises' on their own. For many children, the reassuring presence and support of the teacher is needed, if new learning is to be tackled successfully. When homework involves the collection and collation of information, pupils should be told which sources to consult, rather than be expected to find out for themselves. If preparatory reading is required, then it should be for a clearly indicated purpose with a framework provided by a short list of pertinent questions.

Readability of materials

Can the pupil read at whatever level the material is presented? Does he have the vocabulary necessary to grasp new concepts? Are there too many long words and involved sentences? Children who are withdrawn from English lessons to receive remedial help with their reading are expected to deal with complicated texts in history, geography and science without any additional assistance in those subjects. Apart from the cognitive problems involved, children who are experiencing difficulties in reading may not be able to glean enough information to assimilate new concepts, unless some effort is made to provide simplified synopses and oral summaries of the content of difficult texts.

Matching the reading level of textbooks with the reading age of the children using them is not a difficult task. Harrison (1980) describes the various formulae which are available, explains how to apply them and advises which are most suitable for primary and secondary material. Particularly at the senior level, too little account is taken of whether pupils can read the books from which they are expected to work independently (Lunzer and Gardner, 1979).

Choosing new books may not be an available option. Even if this is the case, much can be done to help pupils cope with unsuitable textbooks containing reading matter beyond their normal level of comprehension. Attention can be directed to relevant paragraphs. Exercises can be simplified or easier activities substituted. Essential concepts can be illustrated by selecting key words which reflect the main ideas from a passage. These can be written up on the chalkboard, explained and discussed before independent work starts. Every effort should be made to ensure that the pupil knows exactly what information to seek and where to find it. Gardner (1980) has coined the acronym DARTs (Directed Activities Related to Texts) to describe this type of approach.

Clarity of presentation

Even pupils who can read adequately sometimes need help in sorting out what they are expected to do. Clarity of presentation should remove any vagueness about the purpose of the lesson or the nature of the work anticipated from the pupils. Are assignments clear enough, so that each pupil knows exactly what is expected? Do some children give up because they do not know what to do? Do others go off on the wrong track, not because they cannot do the work, but because they get the instructions wrong?

Having settled the class into the lesson and taken their minds off other topics, such as the previous lesson, by some quiet seat-work on his own subject, the teacher should introduce new work by giving a simple outline of his lesson plan. This should emphasise what the pupils will be expected to do during and after the teacher's talk, demonstration or film. It is essential to ensure that listening or watching should be active rather than passive. This can be achieved by setting a few questions to be answered or directing attention to important concepts, which are going to be introduced. This also gives an opportunity to check that children have the necessary materials for getting on with their work as soon as the teacher's part has finished.

Instructions should be clearly written on a part of the chalkboard reserved for this purpose, perhaps in a different colour from that used for summarising the lesson content, providing headings and spellings. Regular instructions relating to the presentation and the setting out of work may best be permanently displayed on a poster, with an example of what is required clearly visible.

Checks need to be made that instructions have been understood by asking individuals to repeat them. This should be done as pleasantly and patiently as possible, not with the intention of catching anybody out, but rather just to make sure they have got it right.

As work gets under way, the teacher needs to be around to help. If one person is stuck, a quiet personal explanation can be sufficient, but if several pupils are evidently puzzled, then it is best to stop everyone, get the attention of the whole class and repeat instructions, giving extra examples or further demonstrations, if necessary. It is useful to assume that for every pupil who appears to be stuck there is another who, though working with some appearance of confidence, would welcome the reassurance of a further explanation.

Marking assignments

The consequences as well as the conditions of learning contribute to the nature of the classroom environment. The way in which work is marked and rewarded will influence the climate for nurturing positive attitudes. Is marking on a personal or competitive basis? Do rewards for successful work sufficiently motivate the pupils? How often do individuals gain rewards?

Whether external examinations are involved or not, it is important that marks should be related to standards which give the learner a realistic perception of his own ability. However, this does not mean that the less able child should be constantly reminded of his inadequacy compared with other pupils. Competition can sometimes play a useful part in stimulating effort, but this can be related to individual targets, rather than comparative performances. The same rewards can be given for one child who gets five sums correct and another who gets ten correct, provided that in each case it is a 'personal best'.

It is sometimes helpful to separate marks for content and presentation. This enables the teacher to find something to praise, whether it is getting the idea or setting out the work. Written comments can soften the blow of a poor mark and show that effort and industry are appreciated as well as competence.

Whenever possible, correction should be an opportunity to improve a mark, rather than an imposition or punishment. 'Fair copy never won fresh interest' and it is better to give further practice with new though similar work, always assuming that the first attempt was a best effort; if not, then the mild punishment of repetition may be appropriate.

Successful work may bring its own rewards. Bruner (1966) describes 'intrinsic' motives for learning, which do not depend on rewards outside the instructional activity itself. Children work to satisfy their natural curiosity or for the sense of achievement which follows competent performance. They work for the pleasure of interaction with a well-liked teacher, often identifying with his attitudes and enthusiasms. They work also for the enjoyment of shared effort in being a member of a co-operative group. On the other hand, Skinner (1968) argues that learning depends not on the activity itself, but on the consequences which follow. Children work for 'extrinsic' motives such as praise, approval or more tangible reward, or they work to avoid unpleasant consequences such as disapproval or punishment.

Without taking sides in this continuing debate, the teacher may draw on either theory in developing a positive approach. What matters is the need for an accurate perception of what motivates particular pupils in particular lessons. It is also important that each individual has a regular opportunity of experiencing reward, whether in terms of self-esteem, with the regard of others, or the enjoyment of pleasant consequences.

Behaviour does seem to be better and the atmosphere brighter where ample praise is used in teaching. Praise needs to be natural and sincere and should never become dull and routine. It is a good idea to try to think of at least six synonyms for 'good' and to use them appropriately. 'Great', 'superb', 'fine', 'splendid', 'remarkable' are some examples, or use more colloquial expressions such as 'ace', 'knockout', or 'cracker', if they come naturally. Similarly, 'nice' is a word so often used, when children would surely be more stimulated to know that their work was 'delightful', 'imaginative', 'beautiful', 'interesting', 'original' or 'fascinating'.

Thus far discussion has focused on approaches to classroom management designed to promote a pleasant and positive atmosphere. Next attention turns to considering how to deal with negative attitudes by reducing sources of friction.

Chapter 3

Reducing sources of friction

In any lesson there is some potential for pupil disruption. In recent years, the growth of mixed-ability teaching, often necessitating group work, has increased that potential. Teachers today are therefore more vulnerable to time-honoured ploys, which children have always used to gain distraction from their work. The four main sources of friction are characterised by Francis (1975) as noise, equipment, movement and chatter. None of these sources, by themselves, are a major challenge to the teacher's authority, but each if wrongly handled, can develop from a minor irritation into a major confrontation.

MINOR IRRITATIONS

Noise, for example, might involve shuffling feet or papers, shifting of desks or scraping of chairs, unnecessary coughing or, in one of the worst manifestations, what might be described as wilful flatulence! Even attempting definition indicates how petty the offence is and how difficult it is to frame an accusation concerning it.

Equipment loss or induced malfunction is another potent source of disruption, particularly with the excellent opportunities provided for the display of injured and exaggerated innocence. Protests that 'I did have a ruler, but someone's taken it', or 'I can't help it, if the pencil keeps breaking' can be especially irritating, if the teacher feels the class shares his suspicion that this is a contrived event.

Movement is inevitably more of a problem now than in the days of static sessions of 'chalk and talk'. With more fluid group activities, there is a temptation to wander off for a gossip and a giggle. When apprehended, patently false claims to have been in search of material or pretended fascination with the work of another group add to the teacher's sense of being subtly provoked.

Chatter too, presents more possibilities for dispute in an educational setting which encourages children to comment on their work, than in an era where talking except in answer to a teacher's question was simply prohibited. Once the pupils' right to discuss together the work in hand is conceded, even encouraged, then the volume and relevance of what is said can easily become matters of contention.

Having used such ploys themselves quite recently, young teachers are prone to over-react. Sensitive to the challenge which is there, albeit minimally at first, fearful that they will be thought an easy mark, if they do not take up the challenge, and mindful of their own opinion of 'weak' teachers, they often respond with dramatic and would-be-draconian harshness, which is counter-productive.

Some of these problems can be avoided by giving careful thought to the assignment of responsibilities for the distribution and collection of equipment. Marland (1975) suggests keeping a note on the chalkboard of items such as brushes or scissors given to particular groups, with the name of the person responsible alongside. Similarly, rules can be established to regulate movement and chatter by limiting walking and talking to particular parts of the room. Establishing a few essential rules and clarifying what is acceptable conduct is often sufficient to avoid problems arising, for, as Lovitt (1977) points out, most children 'if they know what we want them to do, will do it'.

Such precautions will not prevent the calculated provocation or deliberate affront, although they will deter the casual transgressor. Even when quite certain that misbehaviour is intentional and provocative, the teacher must be wary of too strong an immediate response. Anger, even if simulated, uses up too much adrenalin and using heavy punishments for minor infractions leaves nothing in reserve for more serious cases. Rather, the teacher should look for a series of responses which are cool, calm and carefully calculated.

MANIPULATING SURFACE BEHAVIOUR

Although derived from their treatment of maladjusted boys over thirty years ago, Redl and Wineman's (1952) amusing description of 'techniques for the manipulation of surface behaviour' still provides a useful framework for discussing appropriate responses to milder manifestations of misbehaviour.

At this stage, misbehaviour is most likely to result from seeking attention, escaping from boredom or warding off inadequacy. It should not be seen as a battle for power or an attempt to gain revenge, although these motives may soon become involved if the situation is mishandled. With tongue fairly evidently in cheek, Redl and Wineman use some amusing bits of pretentious-sounding jargon to describe how teachers handle problems which are 'on the surface', rather than deep rooted.

Planned ignoring

Some provocative behaviour will rapidly exhaust itself unless attended to by the teacher. As noted above, it is often difficult anyway for the teacher to attend to some misbehaviour without sounding foolish. Indefinite noises, muttered imprecations and parroting instructions are examples of actions best met initially by selective deafness or blithe indifference.

However, the emphasis must be on planned ignoring, rather than just hoping the nuisance will go away. Deafness, for example, must be credible in the circumstances or it will merely embolden louder attempts to provoke a reaction. Pretended lack of awareness of the undesirable behaviour should be linked to positive attention to the work in hand.

Signal interference

If apparent ignorance is not working, the next stage requires an attempt to inhibit the unacceptable behaviour by making it clear that its source has been spotted. This signal should block further malpractice, rather as one radio station might jam another by providing 'interference'.

Once eye contact has been made, the teacher's signals may take the form of gestures such as using a frown, raised eyebrows, a shake of the head, or a wave of an admonishing forefinger. Often the signal may involve a quiet, personally addressed request to desist. What is most important is ensuring that the signal is received. As Long and Newman (1976) point out, some children would have you stand and look at them all day without it helping to control their behaviour one bit.

It is also vital to see that the signal is not perceived as a distress signal! The apparent success of verbal criticism and prohibition can easily lead teachers into the trap of believing that nagging works. As quiet admonitions become louder reprimands, teachers can rapidly find themselves at the yelling stage (Poteet, 1973). Once at this point, control and dignity are easily lost. Teacher-baiting is probably the only blood sport widely accepted in modern society, and once the scent of hysteria is caught the most placid and well-intentioned children will join the hunt!

Proximity control

If a signal has failed, restlessness and excitement may be calmed by the physical proximity of the teacher. Just by being close at hand, the teacher can provide a source of protection and orientation. Most children will stop irrelevant activity and chatter and resume their work once a teacher is near. If they do not, then a more serious problem presents itself!

To be successful, 'proximity control' needs to be tried at an early stage, before misbehaviour has got very far. It also needs to be associated with 'interest boosting'.

Interest boosting

The teacher's attention and display of interest in a child's work can refocus attention. Intervention should be specific, rather than general. For example, 'Have you remembered to pay back?' rather than 'How are you getting on with those sums?'.

Marking work done so far is an easy way to intervene, offering help with the task, rather than confrontation over behaviour. This implies an assumption, which is often true, that distraction has resulted from inability to cope with required work.

Marking may give an opportunity to praise and remotivate: 'All correct so far', or 'That's an interesting start to your story'. It may be necessary to demonstrate, especially if little work has actually been done. 'Let me show you again how to set these sums out. I'll put them in your book, then you fill in the answers'. This gives the teacher a chance to modify the difficulty of the task.

Sometimes an alternative activity can be suggested: 'Leave that question for now. Trace the map instead'. Obviously the alternatives should be relevant to the topic being taught, and the difficult task is deferred, not avoided. Otherwise the pupil merely learns another useful work-avoidance technique and sees the alternative activity as a reward for messing about.

Hurdle help

With many children 'interest boosting' will merge with the technique described as 'hurdle help'. For some pupils, particular lessons will present immediate problems, or hurdles, which they cannot surmount without assistance. Unless helped, these children will rapidly become frustrated and fractious. Once aware of their problems, the teacher can make sure that they get early individual attention when approaching an area of difficulty.

Some children may need help in reading through a problem, some need more help with spelling, others will need reminding about how to set out their work. The teacher's tactic should be to provide some assistance, not to collude at avoidance. Initially, it may be appropriate to do some work for the child who is floundering, but the aim is not to remove the hurdle so much as give a push to help him over it. Thus the child with a particular problem with spelling can be helped with key words, but also encouraged to use a dictionary.

Tension decontamination through humour

When there is a confrontation between teacher and pupil, it is as if the classroom atmosphere becomes contaminated by the invisible poisoned gas given off by anger and tension. The air can be cleared by a well-timed joke or comment which draws attention to the funny side of the situation.

Such responses are spontaneous by their very nature and cannot be planned. Humour differs from place to place and time to time. What one group of children might consider a sharply amusing aside, another might find hurtful and sarcastic. Perhaps the essential feature is the ability of teachers not to take themselves too seriously. Long and Newman (1976) illustrate this technique by quoting a teacher who upon discovering an unflattering portrait on the chalkboard, comments on the good likeness, but adds 'you forgot my glasses' and, picking up the chalk, proceeds to draw them.

Hypodermic affection

Coping with anxiety and frustration can be helped by an 'injection' of praise or affection. The teacher needs to make sure that the needle with which this injection is administered is not a blunt one. In other words, for this technique to work it is essential that the praise is valued and the affection is appreciated. With some children, being singled out for praise in front of their friends can have a negative rather than a positive effect. Affection, too, can be a problematic concept. What is intended here is the need to convey a genuine liking rather than a cloying sentimentality. In a classroom where praise is frequent and the teacher's enjoyment of the company of children is evident, then an extra dose will not come amiss.

Direct appeal

Sometimes developing trouble can be averted by the teacher making a direct appeal to the pupil's sense of values. Although it would be cynical to suggest that children today lack a sense of co-operation, fair play and kindness, these values are least likely to be held in high esteem by the sort of pupil to whom it may be necessary to address a direct appeal to stop misbehaving. It might also be argued that where such values are present, they are least likely to be displayed in a group.

Whether appealing to the individual or the class, the value areas more likely to be responsive to appeal concern a sense of reality, possible consequences and self-preservation. Thus appeals might be made in terms of authority. For example, 'I can't allow you to do that', or of peer reaction: 'If you talk, the others can't hear the story'. As with the most traditional appeal to pupil realism, 'If you don't do it now, we'll do it at playtime', there is a fine line between appeal and threat, and the distinction needs to be clear in the teacher's own mind before he can expect the pupils to understand it.

The most effective appeal is the personal one made on the basis of a good relationship: 'Do you really think I'm being unfair?' As with injections of praise and affection, direct appeal is a technique best deployed only after getting to know children very well indeed. As Egan (1981) states, it requires 'a great deal of practice and teachers' "savvy"'.

The preferred course of action remains the avoidance of tension or disruption. Rather than the intervention at the individual level suggested by the last half-dozen techniques, it is often appropriate to rely on organisational or group management techniques.

Restructuring

There are occasions when the best-planned lessons can begin to go wrong. Excitement, noise or disruptive action can build up to such an intensity that teachers feel the need to change to a different quieter activity.

Routine can help here, too. If the excitement starts to become hysterical during the introductory demonstration phase, then the teacher can move more rapidly than originally intended to the pupil-centred practice activity. Thus a worksheet planned to follow a discussion may be brought out earlier to replace discussion, if the class is too noisy or too distracted to concentrate.

Sometimes material proves more difficult than teachers expect. Sometimes individuals seem intent on disrupting loosely structured activities. Sometimes a whole class, or most of it, will have an off day when communal silliness breaks out. (Without backing from any known research, many teachers assert that this usually happens around the time of the full moon!) Whatever the reason, teachers do often need to resort to the technique Redl and Wineman (1951, 1952) refer to as 'restructuring'.

The danger with this approach is the tendency for teachers to threaten children with practice exercises like sums or worksheets, when these are intended to be pleasurable and intrinsically motivating experiences. Also, the children who are least able to handle the comparative freedom of discussion or experiment are quite likely to prefer the regulated familiarity of mechanical arithmetic.

More usefully, this technique is employed in bringing forward more easily managed parts of the lesson, without, as it were, admitting defeat. The teacher implies that, even if incomplete or unsuccessful, the work done is not totally unsatisfactory. For example, 'We'll discuss this topic again another day, but now I want you to do some written work', or 'I think we'll stop there for today. When the materials are all collected, I want to get on to the next chapter in our story'.

In this way the teacher is indicating that he is still in charge of the situation. He is not shocked, disturbed or overcome by the way matters have developed. Remonstration only leaves some pupils feeling guilty that they have let their teacher down, while others feel a glow of victory at upsetting him.

SELF-EVALUATION

Other techniques described by Redl and Wineman (1951, 1952) include removing distracting objects during lesson time, the application of physical restraint and the brisk removal or 'antiseptic bouncing' of disruptive pupils. These measures relate to conflict and confrontation, rather than the theme of this chapter, which has been concerned with preventing mild misbehaviours from becoming more serious matters of contention between teacher and pupil.

Good and Brophy (1980) strongly urge the importance of projecting positive expectations both for attainment and conduct as a way of enhancing the pupil's self-image:

> Students treated as basically good people who want to do the right thing, whose lapses are treated as due to ignorance or forgetfulness are likely to become the prosocial people they are expected to become. Students treated as if they are inherently evil or under the control of powerful antisocial impulses, whose lapses are taken as evidence of immorality rather than just as isolated mistakes, probably will turn out to be antisocial, just as expected.

The responses which have been suggested need to be applied flexibly and with frequent self-evaluation. The teacher should relate them to questions about the content and manner of teaching.

Content

Smith (1979) suggests that looking back on lessons teachers should ask themselves:

- 'What worked today and what didn't?'
- 'Was the work too hard or too easy?'
- 'Was there enough variety and change of pace?'
- 'Were there enough alternatives to fall back on?'
- 'Was there enough revision? Did I repeat, rephrase, refresh, restate the concepts, vocabulary and information?'
- 'Did I ask the right kind of questions?'

Manner

The questions suggested by Smith (1979) concerning manner are:

- 'Did I give enough attention to positive behaviour?'
- 'Did I give too much attention to negative behaviour?'
- 'Did I ignore too much or too little?'
- 'Did I fuss or nag too much?'
- 'Did I praise sufficiently?'
- 'Was there enough humour in the lesson?'.

Answers to these questions will help teachers pitch lessons at the right level of difficulty and preserve a pleasant and peaceful classroom atmosphere.

Part II

Mediation

Chapter 4

Counselling and discussions with disruptive pupils

INTRODUCTION

In Part I of this book the suggestions made to teachers about their management of pupils focused on those strategies which would either prevent, or significantly reduce, incidents of disruptive behaviour in their classrooms. Teachers, however, know well that in their best prepared and well presented lessons, in which they deploy the strategies outlined in the opening chapters, they are likely to encounter some disruptive pupils whose unacceptable behaviour is too frequent and persistent. Some of these disruptive pupils may have the problems of adjustment as these are described in Chapter 5, but this is not true of all of them. Their teachers sooner or later find themselves wondering why such pupils behave as they do, and why it is that they seem to find disruptive behaviour more rewarding than co-operative behaviour and what may be done to make their customary management strategies effective. It is in these circumstances that a teacher may make up her mind to have 'a quiet talk' with a pupil whose disruptive behaviour frequently upsets her classroom.

DECISIONS ABOUT COUNSELLING DISCUSSIONS

It is this 'quiet talk' which is to be explored in this chapter with the suggestion that it might move towards the counselling approaches that Wolfgang and Glickman (1986) describe. In their book *Solving Discipline Problems* the authors include material from Gordon (1974), Harris (1969), Raths, Harmin and Simon (1980), Glasser (1975) and Dreikurs and Cassell (1972) which is a useful guide to a teacher in her discussions with a pupil about his disruptive behaviour.

Here it is important for a teacher who decides that it would be appropriate to discuss the behaviour of a disruptive pupil with him, to be clear about just what it is that she intends to do. She is not going to attempt 'counselling' as understood by trained and experienced school counsellors. She is not going to ignore the school pastoral care service or usurp their functions. Indeed, she intends to tell her colleagues in the pastoral care service what she is going to do and she will ask their advice when she thinks this is necessary.

This is a legitimate decision for a teacher to make. What she wants to do is to overcome the difficulties the disruptive pupil presents without referring him to somebody else, such as the head of house. It is in her lessons that the pupil is disruptive, she knows what he does when he disrupts her lessons, and the circumstances when the disruption occurs. She does not get on well with him, but in their frequent interchanges some sort of relationship has developed; it is not the sort of relationship that she has with the majority of pupils in her class. She believes that if she could improve her relationship with the disruptive pupil, his behaviour would improve. So far as she has observed him, and from what her colleagues have told her, although there is general agreement that the boy is usually a pest and a nuisance in most lessons, he is not hardened and unapproachable.

This awareness of the nature of the task she is to undertake is important. There are some disruptive pupils for whom counselling or discussions, making appropriate use of insights and strategies used by counsellors, are not appropriate. Unless there is some indication that the pupil wishes to change his behaviour and that he is not content to continue with the unsatisfactory performance that has characterised his classroom interactions, what the teacher envisages will not bring about changes in behaviour. Some disruptive pupils are content with their behaviour, and despite what appears to the teacher to be obvious disadvantages to them, they are content to continue in the ways they know. For them it is rewarding. They are indifferent to punishment because they have no real relationships with staff who have to resort to it. They do not care what most other pupils think about their disruptive activities, and they console themselves with the knowledge that although they are not generally popular, they appeal to kindred spirits who consider them to be 'cool' or daring. They are open about their negative evaluation of what the school can offer them and view their time in it as some kind of sentence which they endure, enlivening the time with what distractions they can. For such pupils, the best chance of bringing about some modification in their behaviour lies in the use of more direct methods of control, and in this, Wolfgang and Glickman's book is a most useful resource as the authors describe the strategies that Dobson (1970) has brought to teachers' attention. The key consideration is not which methods are better than others, but which form of intervention is most appropriate for which kind of disruptive pupil and which intervention most appeals to those who make use of it. Unless teachers find that they have their hearts in whatever form of intervention they adopt, no intervention is likely to succeed.

In the present case, the teacher has decided to adopt a counselling – discussion strategy. It is true that she is not an experienced counsellor, but she does have skills which she will need. She knows the importance of listening to children, she knows how to talk to them and how to stimulate them in conversation and discussion. She can recognise signs in pupil behaviour which suggest that they are not telling her the truth, or that they are embarrassed and uneasy. She has enough experience of pupils to know when they are sincere and serious when talking to her. She knows about the school world and is in a position to verify what accounts of it a pupil may describe to her. These are not all the skills and information that a teacher in a counselling role requires, but having them certainly helps.

There is one practical matter about which the teacher has to make a decision – the timing of her counselling discussions. Initially she has to convey to the pupil that she does not intend to continue putting up with his behaviour, that she believes he can alter it and that she is ready to help him do this. In this she has the initiative, because she can indicate that she wants a word with him, putting this firmly but positively. The pupil then does have the impression that it is a matter of choice whether he keeps the first appointment she makes, but that further appointments are likely to be more difficult to arrange. Teachers are now busier than ever because of the many demands upon their time which have followed in the wake of the implementation of the National Curriculum and the proliferation of meetings and commitments to colleagues. If she decides that her discussions with the pupil will be outside school hours, then other complications arise, one of them being communication to the pupil's parents about his delayed departure from school. Another complication is the danger that such an arrangement will be seen by the pupil as a form of punishment, some kind of detention. If this arrangement is the only solution to the problem, then that is unavoidable, but if the discussions are such that the pupil finds them rewarding, this objection will gradually lose its force. It may be that, in consultation with other staff members, the teacher can see her pupil during a lesson when she is not teaching herself and when neither the pupil nor the lesson teacher will resent him missing that particular lesson. If he is a nuisance in other lessons, this may be an attractive proposition to the teacher concerned. Whatever the difficulties of arranging times for the discussions, they will be overcome if they are given enough priority by the teacher herself and her colleagues. Once an initial meeting has taken place, subsequent times for others can be discussed with the pupil. This is a positive feature, for it indicates to him that he is to have some say in a making a decision about the use of his time. It emphasises that consultation and agreement are features of the proposed endeavour.

PROGRESS IN THE DISCUSSIONS

The teacher should be clear about the aim of the discussions. Plainly this is that the pupil should change his behaviour in class, but as this is pursued in the discussions, goals may appear which, if given undue attention, may hinder progress towards meeting the aim. Consideration of these complications is delayed until later on in the chapter, but on starting out, the teacher should keep the aim in view. As an initial step towards it, as there are features of his disruptive behaviour which are recent enough for both her and the boy to recall, exploring one of these gives them both firm ground from which to work. In doing this, she would be following suggestions that Redl (1959), Gordon (1974), Jones (1984), Dreikurs and Cassell (1972) and Glasser (1969) have made. In exploring a well remembered disruptive incident, these authors emphasise that it is the pupil's present situation that is the proper focus of a counselling intervention of the kind that a teacher is equipped to manage. In bringing such an incident to their attention, the teacher should avoid further criticism of the pupil's behaviour which would put him on the defensive and make it probable that he will make excuses for what he did. This would obscure what the teacher is setting out to achieve, which is, that through frank discussion the pupil would understand how inappropriate his behaviour has been, how it has affected other people – herself included, and that together they can find ways of avoiding its repetition. Without labouring the point, the teacher can convey that the pupil is the chief loser in disruptive incidents and the chief beneficiary of altered behaviour. While the teacher should make it clear that she is not unduly concerned with the pupil's excuses for his misbehaviour, she can make good use of them. If, for example, he says 'Well, switching off the overhead projector was not my idea, Douglas suggested it'. This gives her a very good opportunity for what Glasser has called 'door opening questions'. She may ask, 'Why do you think that Douglas suggested that *you* did it?' and ignore his peripheral comments, such as his proximity to the switch and repeat her question – 'Why you?' Her intention here is to draw the pupil's attention to the possibility that some of his disruptive behaviour is due to his wish to be popular with Douglas and others like him, and this suggestion could be explored. He may not make that excuse, but say 'The lesson was boring'. This would give the teacher an opportunity to make the pupil aware of the reality of the classroom situation – that learning cannot be a continuous round of interest and pleasure. (At the same time of course, such an excuse may prompt the teacher to consider whether she may not be able to improve her own classroom performance along the lines suggested in Chapter 2). Another aspect of this classroom reality could also figure in the discussion – that as there were other pupils in the class who wanted to learn, he had no right to prevent them doing so.

The teacher's question 'Why did you switch off the projector' may not turn out to be as fruitful as she had hoped, for the boy may make that well known response, 'I don't know'. This need not be a deadlock, for she can suggest some reason herself, saying 'I think you did it to make me angry' or 'Make me look foolish' or 'Show the class how daring you are'. She may go on 'I think you like these battles with teachers you know – you remember that trouble in the biology lesson last week – you were lucky not to be suspended over that. We had better have a look at what seems to me to be your need to upset teachers and score off them'. In proceeding like this, the teacher is declaring her correct belief that behaviour, however unacceptable or unpleasant, is goal directed, a point which Glasser and Dreikurs emphasise.

In these examples of possible exchanges in a discussion, with a disruptive pupil, the teacher will not go far wrong if she keeps clear in her mind:

(a) that as the discussions are an appropriate intervention, they are worthwhile, and that she is committed to their processes and outcome;
(b) that in them she should demonstrate a concern for the pupil and his future in the school;
(c) that from the tone of her remarks, the pupil is aware of this concern;
(d) that the discussions are ones which demonstrate to the pupil that she believes that he is capable of making reasonable and intelligent contributions to them;
(e) that she is ready to accept that the pupil may bring to her attention features of her behaviour in the classroom of which she is unaware, or has not considered important;
(f) that she keeps the realities of the classroom situation before the pupil, and intervenes when he overlooks them or distorts them;
(g) that she expects the pupil to arrive at some solution to the difficulties that his disruptive behaviour presents, and that she, as a resource, is willing to help him find an appropriate strategy;
(h) that once a strategy has been agreed between them, she shares with him responsibilities in implementing it. Included in her responsibility is communicating to her colleagues what this strategy is and asking them to co-operate in the implementation when and where this is appropriate. Similarly, she should see to it that other members of the class know about what strategy has been agreed, so that they will not put obstacles in the way of the pupil's intention of changing his behaviour.

THE TEACHER'S AWARENESS OF HER ROLE

Once the discussions are fairly under way, it is probable that the pupil will bring into them some features of his behaviour which might suggest to the teacher that she should attempt to help him sort out difficulties which do not originate in the classroom, but are linked with events and experiences outside school. These may be his difficulties with his parents or his recollections of past events of his family. Here she should be very cautious because it may lead her either to go beyond her role boundary, or to become involved with material which she is not equipped to understand or assess. In her discussions she is not assuming the full counselling role. She has not had the training and experience to enable her to work with *all* the material her pupil might bring to her attention and to make use of it. If she attempts to unravel the pupil's account of family events and his experiences with what appear to be uncaring or ineffectual parents or irresponsible siblings, she will inevitably find herself out of her depth, and only too likely to hinder progress towards meeting her aim. This aim is limited to helping the student alter his behaviour and in pursuing it she should stick with what she knows and what she can manage.

She cannot, however, brusquely dismiss the pupil's remarks if he volunteers information about his personal life outside school. Her most appropriate response in these circumstances would be to indicate how they might deal with the information the pupil wishes to pass on. First, she could discuss with him her reasons for not pursuing topics which are beyond the limits of what they can usefully do together. By the time that such topics arise in the discussions, the teacher would have sufficient confidence in the rapport she has established with the pupil to be able to do this without giving him the impression that she is not concerned about his personal difficulties at home. She could then suggest that as their discussions are limited to classroom events, she would, if he so wishes, find a more appropriate person to whom he could speak in confidence about events outside the classroom.

She is fully justified in making such a response. Teachers are teachers, are teachers, are teachers! They should stand firm on their professional base. They are more effective teachers if they can widen that base through their contacts with other professionals concerned with children, and by acquiring through reading and discussion, knowledge and understanding of the skills and insights of others. But this is altogether different from trying to deploy skills where they can only practise as amateurs, as Hanko (1985) emphasises.

But although the pupil does not pass on to the teacher whatever troubles him in his family, she has made a valuable discovery. She is made aware of features in his situation which increase her understanding of him. Awareness that there might be difficulties which he has to put up with at home influences her attitude to the boy. She will not divulge any information to another person which might lead to some enquiries being made without her knowledge of what these are and who is making them, so that her promise of confidentiality is not broken. But with her suggestion that he might find some help from an appropriate quarter if he wanted this, she has increased his appreciation of her as a resource. One positive outcome of the discussion is the pupil's awareness that she could be an approachable confidant should he wish to find help with his personal difficulties. Children who have burdens to bear in their family life are usually hesitant about making these known unless they have experiences of members of staff which assure them that their secrets will be safe with them. The teacher in this case has given her pupil this confidence.

THE GAINS OF THE DISCUSSION

There are gains in the discussions for both the pupil and the teacher. The *pupil* has made an unexpected discovery. The teacher whose lessons he frequently disrupted had extended towards him a concern and an interest he did not expect, and, he believed, did not deserve. In her talks with him he has found that she treats him with respect as an intelligent and reasonable person. This was not quite his perception of himself. Because of his behaviour he had been described as being stupid or doing stupid things, as being a nuisance and a pest for long enough in his school career for him to accept that this was true, and he had fulfilled teacher expectations. So much of what has transpired in his discussions contradicts his self-evaluation. Thus his self-image has improved and he feels good about himself.

It has been a novel experience for him to hear a teacher ask him for his opinions, as has happened frequently in the discussions, culminating perhaps with a question 'What do you think you can do now to alter your behaviour – have you some sort of plan that we could think about?' In answer to this the idea of a contract may have materialised. He may have said 'How about if I promised not to muck about any more – if we had an agreement'. Perhaps the teacher has suggested to him a Behavioural Contract (of the kind described later in Chapter 8), he has agreed and it has been drawn up and put into practice. His behaviour has altered, and he has discovered that he finds the teachers lessons more interesting and satisfying than he had thought likely. He has made more progress since the contract has been operating than in many months before. This has also added to his self-esteem.

He has also been made aware of the possibility that he can find some help with problems in his family if he wants to find it. Until mentioning how his father behaved at home he had thought that he just had to put up with this as best he could. Now he understands that this is not so, and there are people who could help the situation. Taken altogether, the outcome of the discussions is surprisingly good.

There are gains for the teacher as well. First among these is the pupil's improved behaviour and performance. When he altered his behaviour her irritation and frustration with him disappeared. Her concern that others in the class would either be unsettled by his behaviour, or imitate it, also disappeared. She no longer has the anxiety that she previously had, that at any time in her lesson she would have to be prepared to deal with some disruptive incident, which frequently upset her and depressed her.

Besides the alteration in the boy's behaviour, there are more personal gains for her. She has had valuable experiences in her discussions with him, and has extended the range of her professional skills. She has the satisfaction of discovering her ability to manage the few discussions she has had with him, and has brought these to a successful conclusion. She also has the satisfaction that because she now knows more about the pupil, and that he has some kind of difficulties at home, her relationship with him is such that she is pretty certain that he will approach her if he needs help to resolve the problems that these difficulties at home are causing him.

Chapter 5

Confrontation in the classroom: pupils with problems

On the whole it is wise for teachers to avoid confrontations with pupils when these can be avoided, but there are occasions when they cannot be, and there are circumstances when a confrontation is beneficial. A teacher cannot avoid a confrontation, for instance, if she is summoned by a colleague to help in some crisis which had nothing to do with her. The angry pupil may turn on her and continue with her what he began with her colleague. There are some circumstances when a teacher may decide that he is not going to put up with a pupil's provocative or stupid behaviour any longer, or he is going to demonstrate to a pupil who continually bullies or teases others that he has met his match. A confrontation would then be beneficial to the boy concerned, to other pupils who witnessed it, and to the teacher's management. But there are considerations which should guide the teacher in making this decision. If he is convinced that the confrontation would be beneficial he has next to be sure that he can manage it. If, once it has started, the pupil continues to be defiant or provocative, and, if the worst comes to the worst, he has to be sure that he can manage the situation should the pupil attempt to challenge him physically. Once started, confrontations sometimes develop very quickly and unpredictably, so that it is foolish to bring on one and then find that it has gone out of control and escalated into a situation which cannot be managed successfully, so that it becomes an example of pupil hostility and teacher counter-hostility which is demeaning and undignified.

Some teachers, either through tension or inexperience, blunder into confrontations which they do not intend and cannot manage and which are of no value to them, to the pupil concerned, or to those who witness it. Some teachers seek confrontations without proper occasion. These have nothing commendable about them.

AVOIDING CONFRONTATIONS

When thinking about ways in which teachers might avoid unhelpful confrontations, it is useful to consider what it is that upsets the stability of a class of pupils which makes the probability of confrontations greater. There are events which teachers cannot control which do this, such as staff absences which mean that a teacher has to cover for an absent colleague. He does not know the pupils he is unexpectedly called upon to teach, they do not know him, and he is not familiar with the lesson material the pupils expect. An unfortunate aspect of this situation is that the pupils who are difficult to manage are those who tend to be poor at adapting to unexpected changes of routine, or variations in teaching styles. At the same time, there may be pupils who are disappointed that their regular teacher is away and they are going to miss some activity or learning they particularly like.

In these circumstances, it helps to prevent difficult situations from arising if the substitute teacher explains why he is taking the class, and that he recognises that pupils will miss their usual routines, or forego the lesson they had anticipated. Most of the class will not be put out by this unavoidable change, but if there are one or two who may, this preamble reduces their resentment or disappointment. In any circumstances when the stability of a class is at risk, it pays teachers to be careful in their interactions with pupils who cannot cope with unexpected change.

It is not only pupils whose functioning is impaired by changes to usual routines. They may frustrate and exasperate teachers themselves so that they are less able, or less prepared, to bear with unacceptable behaviour. Such negative situations are very often the antecedent events which trigger confrontations.

As we shall see in Chapter 9 the ways in which very anxious or tense teachers interact with pupils are also likely to upset the stability of a class, although they may not be aware of this. The steps which such teachers can take to reduce or avoid this anxiety so that they do not blunder into confrontations, will be described in Chapter 6.

It is not only unavoidable events or inappropriate teacher behaviour which upset the stability of a class, increasing the probability of confrontations. Certain pupils have marked tendencies to do this, and are notorious for their disruptive or attention-seeking behaviour. Among them are pupils with emotional and behavioural difficulties; pupils who take on a role that fulfils the expectations of a class; unpopular or 'victim' pupils and pupils who do not so much disrupt lessons as sabotage them.

PUPILS WITH EMOTIONAL AND BEHAVIOURAL DIFFICULTIES

Behavioural psychologists have helped teachers to understand that many incidents of disruptive or unacceptable behaviour tend to be specific to particular situations, to particular individuals and to particular environments (Ullman and Krasner, 1965; Leach and Raybould, 1977; Hallahan and Kauffman, 1978; Roe, 1978). They emphasise that features in an environment, acting as contingent events to behaviour, either reinforce the behaviour or extinguish it. This explanation has helped teachers to recognise that much unacceptable behaviour is not 'within child', and that they themselves can order classroom environments that will significantly reduce the probability of disruptive behaviour and increase the probability of successful learning and social progress. Application of the principles of applied behaviour analysis and the use of behaviour modification techniques such as those to be described in Chapter 8 have undoubtedly helped teachers to find ways of establishing effective methods of classroom management.

Excellent as these techniques are, it is important for teachers to recognise that many pupils whose disruptive behaviour is a persistent problem, have had experiences of other people and of themselves which go a long way to account for their difficulties in the classroom. This is not to deny that the actual classroom environment may or may not increase their tendency to misbehave, but rather to emphasise that there are causative factors outside the control of teachers which influence these pupils to be the centres of instability in the classroom. It is what these pupils bring with them from their pasts, from previous school experiences and previous personal experiences which bear upon their contemporary attitudes and performance. Their need for counselling and support, for assessment of their problems at home, help for their parents and the involvement of personnel from outside the school, testify to the fact that their problems are not of management of behaviour alone, essential as this is.

Among disruptive pupils are those whose experiences of parent figures have led them to regard themselves as unworthy and undeserving. Because they were not wanted or loved they have not been esteemed by those whom they legitimately expect to esteem them. Consequently they do not esteem themselves, they have negative self-concepts, and we know that a negative self-concept is a serious bar to successful achievement. The experiences of alienation and of failure, not only in school-based learning tasks, but in their relationships and in many social situations, are just the negative experiences many disruptive pupils have had. Their lack of security makes them resentful of criticism; they are not much influenced by punishment because over-familiarity with it has made them indifferent to it. Although some pupils who have had long experiences of neglect and deprivation, will actually seek it, punishment does nothing to alter their behaviour. Indeed, it is just as likely to increase the probability of unwanted behaviour because the punishment, unpleasant though it is, is at least attention.

The experiences such pupils have had affect them in other ways. Not only do they perceive themselves as unworthy and unsuccessful, they also tend to perceive adults in authority as potentially uncaring and hostile. This perception has developed because of their experiences of the behaviour of hostile and uncaring adults in their past which has led them to displace the hostility they feel towards these adults on to teachers, especially when teachers frustrate them, as they have to when they control them. Most pupils, however much they may protest, usually accept criticism or punishment as fair, and are able to make the connection between their offence and the punishment it brings about. But it is not wise to make this assumption about disruptive children who have problems of adjustment. Because they have not been able to trust others, and because their relationships have been impaired by injustice, hostility and rejection, they are likely to regard punishment as evidence of vindictiveness or spite. Redl (1971), and Redl and Wineman (1951, 1952) have given illuminating accounts of the attitudes that over-punished and emotionally disturbed pupils have towards teachers who they present with difficult problems of management.

Mention has already been made of discipline as an inter-personal matter. Teachers agree that they have little chance of managing classes successfully unless they are able to establish positive relationships with most of the pupils in them, and hopefully, with all of them. The pupils who cause the worst trouble in schools are so often those with whom the staff complain that they are unable to make meaningful relationships. It is a feature of many pupils with emotional and behavioural difficulties that they find the making and sustaining of good relationships with others difficult, and some never succeed in doing this.

They are either selfish or inconsiderate, or unapproachable and remote, or demanding and impetuous. They give way to temper and to anger which other pupils find unpleasant or frightening. They are wary of making relationships with adults because their relationships with some of them have caused them much pain and disappointment in the past when they were let down or rejected outright. When they have evidence that a teacher is friendly and caring, that he is predictable and reliable, then many of these pupils react positively and their behaviour improves. But this does not always happen. When there has been persistent and damaging emotional deprivation, some pupils exhibit their most unattractive and demanding characteristics towards a teacher who demonstrates concern and patience. This seems to be paradoxical and self-defeating behaviour, and it is wounding and perplexing to the teacher concerned. At the conscious level, it seems that the pupils are declaring that they have heard expressions of goodwill before, but as this goodwill is rapidly withdrawn when they make demands upon it, they will see how the teacher will stand up to their demands. They then proceed to make these demands, sometimes taking care to direct them towards whatever vulner-abilities the teacher has disclosed in his behaviour. It is when this happens that teachers are heard to remark that they have tried being kind and patient and it did not work. This is unfortunate for both the teacher and the pupil. The teacher takes the pupils' reaction as evidence that his initial approach was mistaken, and the pupils take it as evidence that they are unlikable and adults are hostile. It strengthens their reliance upon what Redl and Wineman have described as the deprived pupil's delusional system, in which their perception of themselves and others is distorted by their previous experiences. As Roe (1978) puts it, 'They create around them a world which confirms their personal view of it'. The pupils have succeeded in dragging into their contemporary relationships just those features which destroyed previous ones. They have manipulated benevolent adults in behaving towards them as they did not intend to behave. If this process continues, their reactions harden into fixed patterns of behaviour which are not quickly or easily changed.

Sometimes such hostile behaviour is motivated by revenge, as Rudolph Dreikurs (1968) has pointed out. Rejected and deprived children are likely to be prompted by feelings of revenge because of the treatment they have received in the past from those who failed them and acted with hostility to them. Some of them feel ready to take it out on somebody without knowing just what it is that makes them feel bitter or angry. Here the process of displacement is operating, and their angry and hostile feelings alight on teachers because teachers do, in fact, share the parenting role. Some teachers, perhaps more usually those who teach younger children, are well aware of this. It is not uncommon to hear them refer to the pupils in their classes as 'my children'. The phrase 'in loco parentis', although this is not used in connection with the feelings in teacher–child relationships, nevertheless bears testimony to teachers sharing the parental role. As this is so, the feelings children have towards their parents are reflected in their feelings for teachers. When these are hostile, but pupils dare not express them towards parents, teachers make very convenient targets for displaced and hostile feelings. Many children with emotional and behavioural difficulties have a limited repertoire of behavioural responses, and from this repertoire they tend to over-use displacement. This fixity of response limits their adaptability. They seem particularly inept at differentiating between people and circumstances so that they behave inappropriately, whereas pupils with more behavioural responses to call upon manage successfully.

There is another explanation for the difficult behaviour many teachers have to bear with and manage as best they can. Some children have learned to behave in the ways that they do, and their learning has been rewarded either by attention or gratification. In the face of disappointment or frustration, they copy or imitate the ways in which their parents or other significant family figures behave. Not only do they witness inappropriate behaviour in models in their environment, they are aware that such behaviour brings its rewards. The father who vents his frustrations at home relies on it to bring him the attention or solace he needs. Siblings who make demands and clamour for attention are given it, and are indulged or gratified according to the frequency, intensity and duration of their demanding behaviour. They themselves are not slow to learn from such models.

Most pupils with emotional and behavioural difficulties are

seriously behind in their learning. They tend to have short concentration spans. Much of the time when they should be listening to what teachers are telling them, or when they should be participating in learning activities, they are either disrupting lessons with some form of attention-seeking behaviour, or their attention is distracted by thinking of unsettling events that take place in their homes. Many of them have marked difficulties in motor control and in perception of printed words or other printed material which interferes with their reading and writing. They may be clumsy and poorly co-ordinated in their movements or hyperactive. Their difficulties in learning and their poor classroom performance is well documented. For example, in their epidemi-ological research in the Isle of Wight, Rutter, Tizard and Whitmore (1970) found a very substantial overlap between severe reading retardation and antisocial disorder amongst pupils in their study. Evidence from the surveys carried out in the Schools Council Project on The Education of Disturbed Children supports these findings of links between disturbed behaviour and poor educational attainment (Wilson and Evans, 1980). Galloway *et al.* (1982) found that disruptive pupils tend to have special educational needs in association with low levels of ability.

Such difficulties directly affect these pupils' behaviour. If they are not actively engaged in learning tasks which they cannot manage and which, in consequence they find uninteresting, they are unlikely to sit passively watching other pupils succeed where they fail. What attention they cannot receive for their successful performance they seek to gain by their unacceptable behaviour. Not being engaged in learning activity they are free to interfere with others who are. Hence such pupils are a considerable threat to the stability of the class, unless they are given a great deal of individual help and attention.

It is likely that there will be more pupils with emotional and behavioural difficulties in schools as the programmes of integration of children with special needs gains momentum. HMI reports testify to this. In 'Aspects of Secondary Education' (HMI, 1979) Inspectors drew attention to the presence of 'highly disturbed and disruptive children' in schools, and in 'Good Behaviour and Discipline in Schools' (HMI, 1986) they comment that some schools have more than their fair share of 'reluctant, disaffected, or disturbed and disturbing children'.

Laslett (1977, 1982), Herbert (1978), Saunders (1979) and Wilson and Evans (1980) have given helpful accounts of the causes of these pupils' difficulties, and indications of how teachers might help them. Not all pupils with emotional and behavioural difficulties are difficult to manage, but many are disruptive and unstable. They find the excitement and the inevitable attention that goes with challenging a teacher temptation that they cannot resist.

PUPILS FULFILLING CLASS EXPECTATIONS

The class wit

In many classes there is one pupil who is the class wit. She is not aggressive or unpleasant to deal with, resentful of authority or uncooperative, and is not set on confronting the teacher, although a confrontation may arise from what she says or does. What motivates her is rather more complicated. It has more to do with her relationships with the class, and theirs to her, than with her relationship with the teacher. Such a pupil is uncertain of her position within the class as status is only usually awarded to a pupil who is a successful and deserving member of the group. Her behaviour and the responses of other pupils to it is governed by the dynamics of group behaviour and in understanding it, it is useful to remember that a class of children does constitute a group. Since she does not have the status that goes with approval given to successful pupils, and wanting to have some recognition and attention, she finds that she can be awarded status through drawing attention to herself by her ready wit and her intrepid display of it. This gives her a good deal of popularity in the class. Her behaviour is less welcome to the teaching staff and has a price which is sometimes exacted, but, on the whole the status and popularity with her peers is worth the cost of the punishments which follow from her witty asides and comments. The role is exciting both to her and to others who enjoy what she does without being involved in any of the unpleasant consequences that sometimes overtake her. She becomes the licensed wit in the classroom, and the description is an interesting one. It is the other pupils who give her this licence, because her behaviour is not without value to them. If she oversteps the limits – if for instance the whole class is punished by laughing too loudly or too frequently at her sallies – they lose patience with her and they withdraw the licence. But usually she manages well enough within the rules as she understands them. The balance she strikes between going just far enough to retain class approval and avoiding their disapproval contributes to the excitement she finds in her role.

As the other pupils encourage and sustain her in her role, it is not easy for her to abandon it, as she may wish to do. When teachers take her to task when her humorous sallies exasperate them, they are not only opposing the girl herself, they are also opposing the other members of the class. What the girl needs is not just criticism or punishment but assistance with her relationship with the other pupils, for if she does attempt to alter her behaviour, they will, by various messages, some overt and some covertly communicated, signal that they want her to continue with it.

The help that the girl needs will be more easily given if the teacher is aware of the dynamics in the class group which sustain her in her role, as Irene Caspari (1976) has made clear. By understanding these, a teacher will reduce the possibility of becoming involved in angry confrontations with the girl who has exasperated her by her humorous interjections, and will be able to help her into a new role. Part of the help will have to be in talking to the class, making them aware of what has been going on, their part in it, and making them understand that they can help the girl to give up her former role by not enticing her to amuse them.

The pupil whose disruptive behaviour satisfies class feelings

There is another aspect of what happens in groups which may account for the disruptive behaviour of a pupil. If a teacher gets on badly with a class and his behaviour stirs up resentment and uncooperative attitudes, it is not uncommon for one bold individual to respond to the prevailing mood and to gather up the feelings in the class and act them out. He shares these negative feelings, and it is his awareness of what other pupils feel, but have not the temerity to express, that gives him the necessary impetus to demonstrate or express them. In this way he is not only acting for himself, he is acting for the class.

In these circumstances, a teacher's criticism or punishment of the individual's misbehaviour is not the most effective way of stopping it. The key to altering the behaviour of the disruptive pupil is to be found in altering the teacher's relationship with the class, by avoiding whatever he does which stirs up their resentment and prevents them from wanting to co-operate with him. While this explanation does not account for all the disruptive behaviour where one pupil continually takes a leading part, it is worthwhile for a teacher to ask himself whether or not the one pupil is doing something which satisfies the other members of the class. If it is, then he would have to think about and repair his relationship with them, and not only his relationship with the disruptive pupil.

The unpopular/victim pupil

In many classes there is one unfortunate pupil who is unpopular with all the others, and while he is unlikely to bring on a confrontation himself he may be the source of exasperation and irritation which upsets the stability of the class. He is frequently teased or bullied and, according to his perception of these events, he is an innocent victim. It is true that many bullies will attack those who are weaker than themselves however their victims behave, but with the perpetually unpopular victim pupil, there are aspects of his behaviour which elicit hostile responses in others. He is unaware that this is so. He knows well enough that he is unpopular, but he cannot account for it. Hostile reactions to his behaviour may arise from his irritating ways, such as his continual interference or the giving of unwanted and usually unwelcome advice. He may make undue demands upon the friendship of other pupils, being possessive of them and jealous of anyone else who may seek to join the relationship. He may be a chatterbox and a sneak, fussy and overdependent, and so muddled in his personal organisation that friendship with him is a burden. Whatever it is about him, other pupils will not tolerate from him what they tolerate in other children. It is this intolerance of his exasperating behaviour that makes him a threat to group stability. He is likely to do or say something which is too much for the self-control of other pupils, so he becomes the centre of angry exchanges in the classroom.

A teacher may best help the pupil, and therefore his control of the class, by pointing out to him that he cannot continue for ever to blame others for his own misfortunes and that he should begin to think about his own behaviour. It is probable that the boy will stoutly deny that any fault lies with him, but he has to be helped to understand that it is his own behaviour that brings troubles on his own head.

A good example of teacher intervention which helped a pupil begin to understand how this victimisation worked was given in a class where Stan, who was generally regarded as a nuisance by his class mates, complained that his sweets had been taken from his classroom locker. The teacher asked who in the class knew that the sweets were there, and discovered that most of them did because Stan had broadcast the fact. Inevitably one of his less honourable class mates had taken them. The culprit admitted that he had done this, and said he would not have done if Stan had not kept on 'showing off about them and getting on his nerves'. How Stan 'got on his nerves' was discussed further, and other exasperating behaviours were described by other pupils. This discussion was painful for Stan and the teacher intervened from time to time to prevent it from becoming too unbearable for him. Fortunately he weathered the storm and for the first time, realised that his own behaviour was responsible for many of his difficulties. When he realised this he was able, with appropriate help from the teacher, to avoid behaving in ways that elicited hostile responses from others.

The situation of pupils with physical, mental or sensory handicap is not quite the same as the unpopular or victim pupil. There is the possibility that such pupils will be teased or shunned, but studies of integration programmes show that this does not happen frequently (Chazan *et al.*, 1981; Hegarty, Pocklington and Lucas, 1982).

The saboteur

There is another pupil who threatens to upset the stability of a class for whom a teacher is well advised to be prepared. This is the saboteur, the pupil who enjoys the drama of a teacher in conflict with another pupil or other pupils, even if he does not escape from such a conflict unscathed. He is not as noticeable as the pupil with more obvious signs of adjustment difficulties and does not engage in openly disruptive behaviour, but he has developed strategies for egging others on towards a confrontation. He will defeat a teacher's intention to ignore unacceptable behaviour by drawing attention to it. He knows just what to say or do when he observes a classroom crisis on the wane so that it will start up again. If a pupil subsides from a temper outburst, he manages to provoke him into another. When he observes a teacher struggling with her irritation, he succeeds in ensuring that she fails in the attempt. A good deal of his subversive and devious behaviour goes on in playgrounds or corridors when no member of staff is on hand to intervene. He is dextrous in avoiding the consequences of his own behaviour and successful in drawing teachers into confrontations.

In managing a saboteur, it is better if a teacher avoids questioning him at length about what he does or has done, because he enjoys the opportunity this gives him to make what capital he can from the situation. If the teacher makes any error in his accusations of his behaviour, then he will seize the opportunity to deny that he did what the teacher knows that he did. One exasperated teacher related the dialogue which followed the late arrival in his class of a girl he had seen minutes earlier combing her hair before a mirror in the domestic science room. When she did arrive, the teacher asked her why she had stopped 'to comb her hair in the mirror'. The girl replied that she had not been combing her hair in the mirror. This flat denial and untruth which she repeated several times during the exchange made the teacher increasingly angry. She at last announced that she had not been combing her hair *in* the mirror because that was impossible. It is this kind of cool and exasperating exchange which demonstrates the dangers of involving such pupils in questioning, and it is better to avoid doing it whenever possible. It is better to tell them what they have done, and to make sure there are no possibilities for ingenious word play. It is also reassuring to other pupils when a teacher does this and demonstrates that he has kept the initiative in squashing someone whose activities many of them have had cause to dislike. It prevents a confrontation from developing which would give the pupil satisfaction.

A knowledge of the behaviour of pupils who threaten the stability of a class is very useful. It goes a long way in helping teachers to avoid conflicts which may easily lead them on to some confrontation that could have been avoided, if they had known more about these pupils (those with emotional and behaviour difficulties); were aware of the group pressures which sustained the class wit in her role; were not taken in by the complaints against other pupils which is characteristic of the victim child; and were quick to take the measure of the saboteur and deny him or her the satisfaction of provoking them, or other pupils, into making hasty responses when exasperated.

Chapter 6

Confrontation in the classroom: teacher strategies

When the variety of factors that affect the interactions between teachers and pupils in classrooms are considered, it is clear that it is not possible to suggest ways in which teachers can always manage to avoid unnecessary or unhelpful confrontations. The most that anyone who is not present in a classroom can do is to point to some guidelines which can help teachers to avoid confrontations which serve no useful purpose and also, as with the confrontation described later in the chapter, to suggest how this might have been more successfully managed once the situation that developed had made a confrontation inevitable. The danger is that when the confrontation between a pupil and a teacher is started by either of them – and when there is tension in a class it only needs one of them to say the wrong thing or do the wrong thing for this to happen – it can easily get out of control with consequences both regret.

GUIDELINES FOR AVOIDING CONFRONTATIONS

Avoiding public denigration of a pupil

Although criticism of some pupils cannot be avoided, it is a mistake for a teacher loudly and publicly to denigrate some offender. This stirs up resentment and hostility if it is frequent, and even if the pupil dare not express this openly, it sours relationships, and is a poor example of adult behaviour. If a pupil is spoken to in a way that demeans him, then he loses face with his peers, and he will seek some way of regaining it when he has an opportunity to put the teacher at a disadvantage. Pupils, especially older ones, resent being 'bawled out' as much as adults dislike it, and they see it as a form of bullying, which it is.

School children are surprisingly unanimous in their comments about what they perceive to be unacceptable behaviour in teachers. They do not mind strict teachers as long as they are not nasty as well (Mills, 1976; Meighan, 1978), and they do not mind being made to work and behave. It is the teacher who speaks to them in contemptuous terms, and who is sarcastic, who frequently brings on confrontations. Marsh *et al.* (1978) in their book *The Rules of Disorder* describe interesting comments that adolescents passed on to them when they interviewed them in their comprehensive school. The boys had rules governing their reactions to what they considered to be fair or unfair teacher behaviour. They credited teachers with authority and expected them to exercise it to provide the right conditions for learning and acceptable behaviour in class. They had little time for teachers who failed to do this. They accepted that criticism or reprimands and punishment, when it was deserved, was legitimate. But if teachers treated them as if they had no status, if they were sarcastic, or punished them unfairly, the boys considered that such behaviour was not legitimate and fell outside the unformulated but mutually understood social contract which operates in classrooms. Then they considered that they were no longer bound by the contract themselves and thus their subsequent disruptive and antagonistic behaviour was legitimated. Their behaviour was then governed by what the authors described as 'the principle of reciprocity'. If the teacher was nasty, they were nasty; if he was insulting, they were insulting; if he considered they were not entitled to respect, they showed him none. They also behaved in accordance with 'the principle of equilibration' so that when they were unfairly put down or denigrated they reacted in a similar fashion to restore their status. Not only did they consider such retaliation legitimate, they felt themselves free to resort to language which teachers would not use.

Ignoring unwanted behaviour

The advantages of 'planned ignoring' of misbehaviour have already been mentioned in Chapter 3, but it is worth while to emphasise that the planned ignoring of some provocative behaviour is not the same as deliberately overlooking it because the teacher cannot do anything else.

Only the teacher in the classroom knows whether he can ignore behaviour or not. It would not have been appropriate for the history teacher to ignore Martin's comment that begins the confrontation described later on in this chapter, for in that situation it would not have led to its extinction through lack of reinforcement, although he might have responded differently to it. Ignoring unwanted or provocative behaviour need not be complete ignoring of it, for a teacher may ignore it when it occurs, and return to comment on it when it is not reinforced by his lack of immediate response. We will see how the maths teacher described in Chapter 7 ignored unwanted behaviour, but he did, when it occurred, look steadily at the culprit for long enough to make him feel uncomfortable and leave him uncertain as to what his later reaction might be. Although this ignoring is not quite what behavioural psychologists usually mean by ignoring unwanted behaviour, it was very effective. However, it went with his whole repertoire of management strategies. A teacher cannot rely upon the effectiveness of ignoring behaviour if he has no other strategies which he can deploy. It is confidence in these strategies which guides him when he decides to ignore behaviour he does not want, and which will extinguish bad behaviour if the planned ignoring needs reinforcement.

Awareness of the effects of non-verbal communications

It is very easy for a teacher, especially if she is angry, to forget the effects that non-verbal communications and body language have on pupils. For some, they show that she is flustered and they take advantage of this; for others, a threatening demeanour communicates a challenge which they take up. Many confrontations begin, or are maintained, not only by what a teacher says, but by the way she walks, or strides towards a pupil, glares at him or points at him. Once a confrontation starts, it is the angry presence of the teacher in close proximity to a pupil that acts as a powerful irritant in the situation and prolongs and sharpens the crisis. From our own experiences, we are aware that we feel uncomfortable if another individual who does not have our sanction to do it, invades our 'private space'. These feelings are aggravated when an angry or unfriendly individual does this – we feel the intrusion more keenly. In the same way, especially with older pupils, a teacher who is obviously annoyed and is not approaching a pupil with any friendly intention, risks making an aggressive response much more probable if she determinedly moves into close proximity to him.

It is doubtful whether enough attention is given to this aspect of teacher behaviour in initial training programmes. Role play would be an excellent way of demonstrating to teachers in training what messages they are conveying by their gestures, gait or demeanour which are often a more accurate indication of their feelings than what they are saying, and have a more immediate effect. Another useful way for teachers to realise how facial expressions and bodily movements are likely to affect pupils is for them to simulate anger or exasperation and walk up to a full length mirror. They could also profit from similar rehearsals while they extend their arms and hands and notice the difference in the effects of those movements, some of them noticeably expressing neutral or positive intentions and some expressing negative or hostile ones. A good deal of effective teaching is theatre, and teachers can learn a great deal from observation of experienced actors.

Avoiding physical interventions

A very common feature of a crisis in the classroom, which makes a confrontation more probable, is a teacher's attempting to grab some object a child has which is preventing him from paying attention or distracting others. In these circumstances, especially if the teacher is bigger and stronger than the pupil, it is tempting for him to make a grab at the personal stereo, or whatever it is that the boy has and has refused to put away, or surrender, when asked to do so.

The teacher may be successful in doing this, but grabbing at the radio, or pushing the pupil aside to get hold of it, moves the situation into a much more unpredictable dimension, and may well become the first step in a confrontation.

The pupil may begin the tantalising manoeuvres of moving it out of the teacher's risk, perhaps by passing it on to others. There is no way of controlling this catch-as-catch-can manoeuvre, and each move in it increases the teacher's discomfort, increases the pupil's satisfaction, and adds to the tension. For the spectators in the class, it is hard to beat as a diverting spectacle. For the teacher, it has few equals as an exasperating and undignified display of impotence. He may succeed in loosening a pupil's grip on the radio, but it then falls on the floor and is damaged. The situation now takes a decided turn for the worse. Although the pupil was at fault in the first place, the damaged stereo has complicated the situation and lessened the distinction between the rights and wrongs of it. If the stereo was a treasured possession, the pupil who owned it may be so incensed by the damage, accuse the teacher of damaging it, and turn on him with language and behaviour that leads to confrontation. In the ensuing conflict, with its unpredictable consequences, the original offence is lost sight of. At the end of it all, the trigger that began the swift march of events was the teacher's physical intervention. This did not cause the crisis – the pupil did that by refusing to switch off or give up the stereo when asked – but the teacher's grabbing moved the crisis into a confrontation.

The Open University film 'It All Depends Upon Your Point of View' demonstrates the dangers of a teacher making a physical intervention. In it we see a teacher go angrily up to a girl to take a fountain pen from her, who raised her hand with the pen in it as she approaches. This hurried action releases a stream of ink from the pen which sprays across the girl's blouse. She looks at it in horror, and shouting 'It's all your fault!' she hits the teacher, or the teacher hits her, or the teacher's face comes into contact with her hand. In the moment of confrontation, brought on by the teacher's attempt to grab the pen, no one knew what happened – who struck whom, who struck first, whose hand got in the way, whose face got in the way. The confusion and panic, which so often goes with an unsuccessful attempt at physical intervention, emphasises that it is better to avoid it.

Reluctance to apologise

It is not uncommon to see a teacher make some blunder in classroom management, perhaps by accusing a pupil unjustly, or snapping at one who is not the real culprit, and to be patently in the wrong, and then compound the error by persisting, when an apology would have avoided a confrontation.

It is not demeaning to make an apology. Teachers are not super people who never make mistakes, especially when they are under stress. If a teacher is really in the wrong, then it is courteous, and it shows respect for pupils, to apologise. If they do not do this, which is what they expect pupils to do when they are in the wrong, it is usually because they have the mistaken notion that if they admit to making mistakes they weaken their authority. The opposite is more likely to be true because pupils respect them for their honesty.

It is better to be open about an apology. To hum and haw, and then say 'Well, perhaps I was in the wrong' is easier than saying 'I am sorry, I was mistaken', but it is less fair and less likely to disarm a resentful and potentially disruptive pupil.

Escalation and detonation in confrontations

We have seen already that there are inevitably some pupils whose behaviour makes a confrontation probable. When teachers know who such pupils are, they can adapt their approaches to them so that they avoid a conflict, or use some appropriate strategy which will reduce the chances of a conflict escalating into a confrontation. It sometimes happens, however, that a teacher will bring about a confrontation with a pupil who is usually reasonably behaved but, unknown to him, has reasons for his surliness or unwillingness to co-operate. He is not aware of antecedent events which affect such a pupil's reactions to reproof or criticism. When this happens, and then the matter is discussed afterwards, then one hears such comments from the teacher concerned as 'If only I had known that she was worried about her sister', or 'I wish I had known that he had that flare up before my lesson'.

The confrontation described below is an ugly and serious one, but not one unknown in many classrooms. The teacher concerned in it made a reasonable request to the pupil, but he had unknowingly stumbled against a boy whose mood at the time, arising from previous events quite outside the teacher's control, made it important for him to avoid making any provocative comments or hasty actions. The teacher's manner unfortunately aggravated the situation that arose in the classroom, and this swiftly moved towards a confrontation that went out of control. The serious consequences were not altogether due to the boy's mood or antecedent events. The teacher made mistakes and the boy contributed his measure of unpleasant behaviour. One of the sad features of the confrontation was that both the boy and the teacher regretted what they had done, but by then it was too late. In his comments on conflicts between teachers and pupils Pik (1981) has drawn attention to the sadness which staff feel when the consequences of some upset in a classroom are more serious than they intended them to be, and these feelings are very real. In some ways ugly confrontations are like accidents. They happen very quickly, and the situations of those concerned in them are dramatically different from their situations before they began.

The boy concerned was reasonable enough in school. He was in the third year, and there was no evidence that he had significant behavioural difficulties. He had the usual uncertainties of mood associated with adolescence, but on the whole he was pleasant and co-operative. However, on the morning of the confrontation, matters had not gone well for him, and the history lesson was a climax in a series of unfortunate events. He had not woken up early enough to go on his paper round, which meant that he was going to have to face his employer's wrath when he next saw him. He was also late for school, and that meant he would be in detention later in the week. He accepted this, but he found the events in the PE lesson, which preceded the history lesson, harder to bear. He had come to school without his PE kit, and that had meant he could not join in the PE lesson, but had to sit on the side watching others enjoy it. He had looked forward to this lesson as a bright spot in a rather dreary day. He had had words with the PE teacher over some trivial misdemeanour and had come off the worse in this encounter. His lateness in getting up and his forgetting of the PE kit were largely due to the rather disorganised home where he lived, but he had cleaned his PE shoes and put his kit ready, and then forgotten it in his hurry. He was cross with himself and disappointed that his preparations had gone for nothing.

He had chosen history as an option in the third year, but more because of the demands of his timetable than his interest in the subject. He was present in the history lessons but he was not a participant in them. The lesson in which the confrontation took place was one in which the teacher talked to the class and then asked them to read passages from their history books. It had been rather a lifeless and dreary lesson until Martin leaned across to his neighbour's desk and said loudly enough for the teacher to hear 'Who cares about the flipping Renaissance anyway?' In leaning across his desk he knocked his history book on to the floor, but this was accidental.

The teacher, who was explaining some point about Brunelleschi's cupola on the church of Santa Maria del Fiore in Florence, was aware that he had only a tenuous hold on the pupils' attention. He was also aware that the lesson had not gone well and that he should have found a more interesting way of presenting his material. He was, in fact, just holding on till the bell rang, glad that this was due in ten minutes. When Martin interrupted his talk, he called out 'What did you say?' He had heard what Martin had said only too well, which accounted for the challenging tone of the question. He had intended to convey that Martin's comment had annoyed him. He certainly did not want him to repeat his remark. Rather, he anticipated that his question would serve as a warning, that the boy would realise that he had heard something unpleasant and he would shuffle out of the difficulty to avoid further trouble. Unfortunately this did not happen. Martin was already sore at the morning's events and was seeking some way to restore his self-esteem. He did not like the history teacher, the challenge in his tone further piqued him, and he was prepared to rise to the challenge. The history teacher was a less impressive figure than the PE master, whose actions in the previous lesson still smouldered. He repeated his remark, loudly and clearly with challenge in *his* voice. It produced a silence that had not hitherto been a feature of the lesson.

Whatever the teacher might have done about the first interruption, when he asked Martin to repeat it, he made a mistake which had serious consequences. He then made another. Now angry at Martin's impertinence, though he had only himself to blame for it, he walked towards him, and looking flustered and angry, pointing his finger, he snapped 'Pick up that book!' The confrontation was now set. Events then followed at surprising speed. The teacher's looks, his movements and demeanour further increased the challenge in the confrontation. He did not overawe the boy, but incited him to further defiance. Both he and Martin were now on the 'escalation–detonation' staircase, and in their continued challenges and responses they drove each other further up it. Martin's response to the command was a surly refusal; he went another step up the staircase. The teacher shouted at him 'Pick it up at once!' – going several steps higher up the staircase. By this time the whole class was aware that dire events were about to happen. The silence had given way to noisy interchanges that encouraged Martin and further discomfited the teacher. He realised that the affair was slipping out of his control, and he was also aware that the noise could be heard in the adjoining classroom. He was now standing over Martin looking flustered and angry and maintaining the tension by his presence so close to him.

When Martin met the command, 'Pick it up at once!' with the rejoinder 'Pick it up yourself!' another feature of the confrontation appeared. Both he and the teacher began to panic. Martin, for all his apparent coolness, had defied the teacher to the point of no return and felt he could not back down and be seen to have been worsted in the encounter – the whole class was watching him with excited interest. At the same time he was uneasy, for what was now happening was unfamiliar to him. He was not a practised disruptive and defiant pupil. The teacher also gave way to panic as he realised the corner into which he had been manoeuvred. He made a last unsuccessful attempt to overawe Martin, despite the evidence that this was unlikely to succeed. His panic prevented him from realising this and what he said was the last few steps up the staircase from which the confrontation detonated. He made a furious verbal assault in passionate terms which he would not normally contemplate using. 'Pick it up! Pick it up! How dare you speak to me like that? You are a lout! You look like one and you behave like one. Pick up that book or I will . . .' No one knew what the end of the sentence might have been, what threat or ultimatum might have followed. When he called Martin a lout, this so stung the boy that he got to his feet in a reflex action in the face of the verbal assault. What then happened was confused and illustrated exactly the way in which tension and panic leads to the misperception of intentions and actions.

Martin stood up. The teacher reached out his hand. What he had intended to do as he explained afterwards, was to put him down into his seat – which was a risky thing to attempt. For a fraction of a second Martin saw this hand coming towards him, and he raised his hand to push it aside. The teacher saw Martin's hand and thought the boy was going to strike him. In self-defence he struck him with his other hand. It was not a heavy blow and it was not directed to Martin's face, but also in self-defence as he said afterwards Martin returned it with a more directed punch which knocked the teacher off balance and cut his lip. In the awful silence that followed, Martin ran out of the classroom. The whole confrontation, from the moment when Martin said 'Who cares about the flipping Renaissance anyway?' to his exit from the room had taken just under a minute. His flight from the classroom, the slamming of the door following the noise of the confrontation, had brought the teacher from the adjoining room to the scene. He did what he could to restore order, the history teacher withdrew to the staffroom, and the lesson fizzled out. At the subsequent enquiry, Martin was suspended for ten days. Both he and the teacher regretted what had happened, but neither would accept the other's description of what had happened when they both raised their hands.

In analysing this unpleasant incident, its whole setting has to be looked at. Although the history teacher's control of the class was not very good, it was not generally disastrous. The most obvious weakness was not so much his control but the dreary and tepid presentation of his material. The diminishing interest in the lesson had a direct bearing on the interruption which led to so much trouble. As has been mentioned in Chapter 3, Redl and Wineman have drawn attention to the need to inject some stimulation into lessons when pupils' attention wanders. The alert teacher picks up these signals and does something to bring their attention back to what he is saying. The history teacher seemed unconcerned about the shuffling and whispering and other signs of boredom in the room until Martin's interruption electrified everybody! The teacher could have done something to keep the interest in Renaissance architecture going. It was in the long period of the pupils' passivity and boredom that the crisis gestated. Crises do not usually erupt without some warning signals. There were plenty of warning signals given out.

It was Martin's comment that began the series of events which led up to the confrontation. The book falling to the floor, which played such a crucial part in it, was accidental. As it was simultaneous with his interruption, it strongly influenced the teacher's reaction. But had he had more success in dealing with it, he might have been able to keep the matter of the book in perspective.

He could hardly have ignored Martin's interruption. Although he should not have said what he did, it was not an outrageous comment. In the prevailing atmosphere of resigned boredom, some other pupil would inevitably have laughed loudly at it, or expressed agreement. But how different the outcome would have been if he had said something which expressed his displeasure at the interruption in more reasonable terms. He could have said 'That will do, Martin. You keep your comments to yourself. Just pick up the book like a good lad and give me your attention for a few minutes'. Or he could have made a more light-hearted comment, such as 'Well, Martin, Bruneschelli's cupola might not sound like your cup of tea, but wait until you see it one day. Now come on. It will soon be dinner time', or even better 'Martin, please do not talk to Fred. What's the matter, anyway? You have been sitting like a bear with a sore head all morning'. This would have given Martin the opportunity to say something about his frustrations during the morning. He may not have taken the opportunity, but if the request had been put in a way that did not slight him, and if 'What's the matter anyway?' had been said with concern and not as a challenge, it is quite probable that he would have responded reasonably. Whatever the teacher said, what was needed was some remark that gave him room for manoeuvre, and not something which reduced this room. Unless, of course, his question 'What did you say?' was sufficient to deter Martin at once. Even with a pupil who had not had the frustrations and disappointments that Martin had had that morning, asking that was taking a risk. The teacher did not know why the boy was so disgruntled, but his loud repetition of what he had said took the teacher past the point when he might have given Martin a chance to say something in mitigation. The repetition of his original comment increased the tension in the exchange, which was already beginning to show in the teacher's challenging tone. It also had another very unfortunate consequence. There was now no chance of keeping the interchanges between him and the teacher reasonably private. The whole class had heard the comment and there was now an alert audience waiting for the next development.

Here the art teacher mentioned in Chapter 7 comes to mind. When she realised that a pupil was attempting to bring on a confrontation with her, she removed her from her audience by sending her to the head of house. In the crisis in the history lesson, there were two protagonists who, between them, maintained the momentum of the confrontation, but the presence of the other pupils added to this momentum, and they influenced both Martin and the teacher. Their presence added to the tension they both felt, and because they were there Martin could not step off the escalation staircase – or he felt he could not. To a certain extent, Martin's behaviour, once he had challenged the teacher, was propelled by the other pupils, and to a certain extent, he was acting out what most of them felt. They were bored with the lesson, but they did not have the boldness to say so. He said what most of them would have liked to have said about Renaissance architecture. He said it because he was bold, because he did not like the teacher and because he was feeling frustrated and wanting to do something to 'keep his end up'. The temptation to do this overcame his usual restraints when he was challenged in front of the class.

Once Martin had repeated his comment, it was clear that he was not going to be overawed, and that he was going to engage the teacher in a power struggle, and that he would match anything that the teacher would contribute to it. The situation could probably have been saved, even after the mistake of asking him what he had said, if the teacher had *stayed where he was* and not increased his challenge by striding towards him and getting into close proximity to him. It was here that his body language emphasised his challenge, and prompted Martin to respond with counter-challenge. And once both of them began to panic, almost inevitably one or both of them would misperceive each other's intention and act precipitately. Neither he nor the teacher could, at that stage, easily retreat from the confrontation, but unless one of them did something to slow down the swift ascent up the escalation staircase, it was certain that they would reach the top of it and reach the detonation point. As Martin showed it was not going to be him who would arrest the ascent, then the teacher should have done it. He was, after all, the more mature of the contestants. The situation was deplorable, but as it had reached the stage it had, all that was left to the teacher was to save his dignity.

Retreating in such a situation is not pleasant for a teacher, but it has to be weighed against the alternative. When he and Martin were eyeball to eyeball, any further provocation was bound to lead to some form of physical encounter, as the pupils watching the confrontation realised – they were waiting for it to happen. In such a physical encounter the outcome would have been unpredictable and only too likely to have serious consequences. At best it would be demeaning and against the teacher's professional code, and at worst it could have had a disastrous sequel for him. Whatever else the audience of pupils might have said about the teacher's handling of the confrontation, if he had avoided physical contact with Martin, they would have recognised that he had preserved some of his adult status by drawing back from a physical intervention.

What the spectators in the class thought about the teacher's behaviour is worth considering a little further. The pupils in the class were adolescents, and not far from entering the adult world themselves. As such, they were interested in the ways adults behave, and they would have been close observers of the conflict, judging the teacher's behaviour not only with reference to the confrontation itself, but more generally as adult behaviour, a point that Fontana (1985) makes in his book on classroom control. It is an aspect of a teacher's task with older pupils – they are under constant observation and assessment, not only as teachers, but also as adults providing those who are near-adults, with models of behaviour. This is even more true of Martin's age group than it was when the history teacher was a pupil himself, because, as demographic research shows, the period of adolescence begins at the age of twelve and is not any longer confined to teenagers (Laslett, 1991).

In their reports, HMI bring another aspect of teacher behaviour to our attention. In 'Aspects of Secondary Education' (HMI, 1979) they make the comment that the resolution of adolescents' difficulties 'may well be regarded as part of the educational process. Young people may be helped by the skills and patience of teachers to work through their own problems and come to a code of behaviour acceptable to themselves and to others'. It would be an exaggeration to say that Martin had exceptional problems, but he did have the difficulty of managing and restraining his behaviour when he was feeling frustrated and annoyed with himself for having missed his PE lesson and having such a bad time before he went into the history lesson. He did not learn much about coping with these feelings from the skill and patience of the history teacher.

Returning to the confrontation itself, it began with a pupil's interruption and an accident. Within sixty seconds it ended in a disaster which neither of the principals foresaw and neither of them wanted. The outcome was out of all proportion to the original offence. Martin should not have said what he did or behaved as he did. But at no time did the teacher allow an opportunity for the momentum for the confrontation to subside. There were opportunities as the tension increased for him to reduce it, and as the older and more responsible partner in the conflict, he should have done so. It would not have been very pleasant for him to retreat from his position, but the alternative was much worse. It was true that as Martin was suspended, he did not 'get away with it'. But no one gave the teacher much credit for the affair, for it was not as if an example had been made of a hardened offender.

The description of this confrontation shows how rapidly difficult situations in a classroom will deteriorate when an initial error in its management is compounded by confused thinking, anger and panic, which combine to propel the participants towards an unpredictable and unwanted outcome.

Chapter 7

Imperturbable, resilient and disruptive teachers

This chapter is concerned with observations of the classroom management of teachers, describing what they actually did or did not do which either prevented disruptive behaviour from occurring, or extinguished the first signs of it, contrasting this with teacher behaviour which elicited resentful and uncooperative reactions among pupils.

From his observations of teachers' interactions with pupils in a comprehensive school, and from his discussions with them, Jordan (1974) was able to differentiate between 'deviance insulative' and 'deviant provocative' teachers. The difference between the 'deviance insulative' and the 'deviance provocative' teachers, and the different ways in which pupils reacted to them, illustrated their different attitudes to pupils and different perceptions of their task. Those whose lessons were rarely disturbed by disruptive behaviour or who managed this behaviour quickly and effectively and insulated it, had positive attitudes towards all pupils. They perceived their task as providing an appropriate learning environment for all the pupils in the class and took care in their preparation material, and in its presentation, so that the demands they made were appropriate for individual pupils. They expected the pupils to work and co-operate, and they, in turn, worked hard and were courteous and responsive. Those whose classes were frequently disrupted by misbehaviour, frequently challenged or provoked pupils, had negative attitudes towards those whom they considered to be deviant and made these feelings plain. They made very little attempt to provide an appropriate learning environment which made it easy for the less able and less well-motivated pupils to succeed; they were frequently discourteous and frequently denigrated pupils.

With effective and successful teachers, their management

techniques so well express their attitudes to pupils that in their teaching style it is not easy to disentangle one from the other: it is not impossible, however, as the descriptions of the mathematics teacher and the art teacher, which are included here, shows. Both of them would fit the description of 'deviance insulative' teachers.

The maths teacher gave the impression that his management was so effective that it would not cross any pupils' minds that they would not co-operate in his lesson – it did not seem to cross his mind that they would not, either. This confidence was one of the keys to his success. The art teacher was rather different. Her management was not so embracing nor as complete, but she shared the maths teacher's positive attitudes to pupils, and she did not let any disruptive behaviour spread from its point of origin to other pupils.

THE IMPERTURBABLE TEACHER

Whenever possible, and he made it possible on a surprising number of occasions, the maths teacher was in the classroom before the pupils arrived. If there were other pupils in the room who had not left to go to other lessons, he usually ignored them. He then cleaned the chalkboard if this was necessary, and sat at his desk. In many lessons he did not get up again until he left the room at the end of the lesson, although he did sometimes walk quietly round the class. His quietness was a noticeable feature of his behaviour. He very rarely raised his voice, and rarely made any gestures, except to point to the chalkboard if he had written or drawn on it.

When the class had assembled they sat down, as they knew that the first half of the lesson was the oral part, when he taught them some new material or took up some unfurnished explanations from his previous lesson. In doing this he asked pupils to comment on what he had told them, he asked questions as necessary, and put these questions to all the pupils in the room. It was noticeable that he spoke to the class as if every member of it had something to contribute to whatever question he raised. There were no 'easy riders' in his lessons! If a pupil said something which was patently irrelevant, or which showed he had not grasped the point, he would look at him with a mixture of concern and slight bewilderment, and then say, 'No, that cannot be right – you have not thought about what you are saying. Listen . . .' and he would put in a few more clues to help the pupil. He did not dismiss any contribution out of hand. If impatience from other pupils showed that his clues were not going to produce the required response, he would say, 'You don't understand. I will try and clear that up with you later'. This was said without reproach, and certainly without threat, and in the second part of the lesson, he would make another attempt.

In the second part of the lesson the pupils did the work set which was an extension of the first part. While they did this he sat at his desk, and asked the pupil who had shown confusion in the earlier part of the lesson to bring his book to the desk. He then gave whatever help was appropriate. It was here that any pupil in difficulties could approach him for any help he needed with the work set.

If pupils talked, he would ask them what was the matter, and waited for an explanation. If this satisfied him, he made some comment which made it clear they should get on with their work. If the explanation did not, he looked at the offender for an appreciable period. This steady gaze was a warning sign that pupils commented on in their descriptions of his lessons. Sometimes nothing followed it, as it was sufficient to deter the offender. But sometimes something did – a sharp reprimand given in a quiet tone, which was not challenging or provocative. Sometimes this reprimand was accompanied by some 'stage business'. He would take out a small notebook and, apparently, write the offender's name in it. There was no direct evidence that every offender's name was in the book. But there was evidence, as any persistent offender discovered later on, if he had too frequently exceeded the limits that were set on behaviour, that all the occasions when he had offended were on record, and restitution was sought. Why some pupils' names were recorded and retrieved and others were not seemed a mystery to the pupils, but it was not. He knew the individuals in each class very well, and knew for which of them further action was needed, and for which of them the appearance of his notebook was itself a sufficient deterrent. As the pupils commented, 'You never knew when he had nicked you – it was best not to risk it'.

It was also in the second part of the lesson that he turned to the homework books on his desk. On top of this was a card with the names of any pupil whose homework book was not included. He would say, 'Jenkins, I do not seem to have your homework – why is that?' This was in the tone of a question put to discover information and it was not challenging or threatening. 'I do not seem to have . . .' implied that he might have made some mistake in his collection and marking of the books. Jenkins' explanation was followed by a request that he should give in his work by a certain time, or by the appearance of the notebook, or both. Whichever way he accepted or rejected the explanation, the work was invariably done.

Below the card with the names of pupils who had not given in their homework were the books of those who needed help. This he provided as far as he could in the time available. The books at the bottom of the pile belonged to pupils whose work was successfully done. When handing them back their books he made some positive and encouraging remarks to them. In the last few minutes of the lesson, and always before the bell rang, he asked the children to stop work and pass their books forward. His last act was to clean the board if he had used it for demonstrations, pick up the piles of books at the end of each row of desks, and sit down. After the bell rang – and certainly not when it was ringing – he told the class to go to their next lesson, he knew what this was and where it was to be held. He would stand by the door as they went out.

The pupils in the third, fourth and fifth years of a secondary school enjoyed these lessons. They commented that he was fair and appreciated his treatment of them as individuals. They thought he was a bit hard, but they also remarked that as he made them work they learned a great deal. One of the noticeable features of his lessons was the amount of work that both he and the class did. In the classroom there was an air of confidence and industriousness. The classroom routine was predictable, and he was predictable. Unsettling events, on the whole, did not happen. If any apparatus was needed, there were monitors to give it out. Only on very rare occasions did he turn his back on the class to look into a cupboard or go into the store room. When he did this, there was usually some increase in the amount of noise, which, on his return, he usually ignored. But the pupils could not count on this, because sometimes he would reprimand them, and sometimes he had recourse to his little notebook.

In considering the effectiveness of the maths teacher, we recognise that he had a lot going for him. He taught a subject he liked to the top streams of older children. He did not have to manage pupils who had to move about to use apparatus or equipment. He had an equitable temperament. But when allowance is made for these circumstances, the fact remains that he was the kind of teacher who behaved in the way Jordan suggested 'deviance insulative' teachers behave, and the kind of teacher whom pupils respect, according to their comments to Harré and Rosser (1975). What was it that he did, or avoided doing, that won him respect?

He respected the pupils. He showed this in the way he spoke to them, and in the way he listened to them. He did not shout at them, or assume they were in the wrong until he had established this – as was shown in his question to Jenkins about his homework. When he had to reprimand someone, he did it quietly and in the same tones as his ordinary speech. O'Leary and O'Leary (1977) have reported a research study showing that quiet reprimands privately delivered are more effective than public ones loudly. He assumed that all the pupils were able to manage the tasks he set and he included all of them in the questions he asked. If any pupil could not answer the question, he showed patience and willingness to give more information.

He also showed respect in the work he set. He knew it would make demands upon pupils but the level he set showed his confidence that they were capable of doing it. The care with which he marked their homework showed respect – he expected them to do it and he devoted a good deal of his time to their efforts.

He was meticulous in his preparations, extending these to small practical details. The monitors who collected the books at the end of each lesson always sat in the front desks. When he turned to the homework books, which had taken him some time to put in the order he wanted, with the books of the pupils he wanted to talk to at the top of his pile, he would not waste time in shuffling through them looking for the one he needed. He learned and remembered the pupils' names. He knew their timetables, so that he could tell them where they went after his lesson. All this took a considerable time – and there was an element of pedantry in it – but the effect on his classes was overwhelming. He always had the initiative, and he always kept it. The timing of the lessons, for example, showed this. He was never overtaken by the ringing of the bell, and he did not have any awkward interval to fill in waiting for it to ring.

There was his demeanour in the classroom. His quiet voice and quiet movements showed that he was in control of himself. His classroom behaviour and his own industriousness gave the clues to the behaviour and performance he wanted. He was clear about the learning environment he wanted, and having made this clear to pupils, he would not let them depart from it, nor would he depart from it himself. This clarity and predictability were enormously reassuring to pupils, and pupils who are learning new or difficult material need whatever reassurance they can get. He provided them with what Fontana (1985) has called 'a cognitive map' to guide them in their learning and behaviour.

He did not give chances for disruptive behaviour to begin. He was in the classroom before the pupils, he did not turn his back on them except to write on the chalkboard, he kept his cupboards in apple pie order and did not have to rummage through them looking for what he wanted. By all this attention to detail, the pupils recognised that they were in the grip of someone whose control was certain and also relaxing. They had only to fall in with his plan, or follow the map in order to please him; pleasing him was more rewarding than displeasing him.

Finally, although he did not seem to recognise this for he never mentioned it, he made use of effective behavioural techniques. He ignored unacceptable behaviour that he regarded as trivial, and rewarded the behaviour he wanted. In the matter of his 'stage business' with his notebook, pupils were not sure, as they commented, 'when he had nicked you – it's better not to risk it'. In behavioural terms, what he was doing was to use negative reinforcement on a variable ratio. Children are negatively reinforced if they do something to avoid an unpleasant or adverse consequence. If, for example, they will only work to avoid being nagged, to avoid the nagging they do their work: they have been negatively reinforced (Vargas, 1977). If negative reinforcement is intermittent, they do not know when to expect an unpleasant experience, so they work or behave acceptably all the time. Their avoidance of an unpleasant consequence is continuous.

Because the maths teacher had little humour, and because of his punctiliousness, he was not the most popular member of staff. But the pupils liked him. He was what Meighan (1978) had described as a 'nice strict teacher'. The older pupils, who had a shrewd appreciation of the differences between effective and ineffective teachers, expressed their gratitude to him for the habits of work he had instilled into them, and for the progress they had made in mathematics.

THE RESILIENT TEACHER

There were noticeable differences between the art teacher and the maths teacher. It was more obvious that she enjoyed working with pupils, she was less meticulous and less restrained. She was more humorous and outgoing. She relied less on non-verbal communications. Whereas the maths teacher would react to unwanted behaviour with a look of surprise and slight disdain, she would use such phrases as 'Don't be such a silly ass'. She would criticise pupils more frequently than he did but she never denigrated them. When she thought it was appropriate to give one 'a proper telling off' she would do this privately. She was enthusiastic about her subject and this spread to the pupils. Because they were free to walk about and to talk during the lessons, she had to manage a less structured situation than the maths teacher. There were more opportunities for pupils to mess about and waste time and materials. She had made the rules that regulated their use of materials and equipment quite clear and would frequently draw attention to these. It was noticeable that the pupils accomplished a good deal in her lessons, and as she moved quietly around the tables she was on hand to encourage them. When she criticised pupils' work, she prefaced it by commenting on what she could praise about it. She made more frequent use of praise than the maths teacher.

Her control of the class was not so outstanding as his. The atmosphere in the art room was more relaxed than the atmosphere in the maths room, and there were one or two children who did not work consistently and who made more noise than she found acceptable. She went straight to them and insulated it quickly. In doing this, her reactions seemed to be on a graduated scale. With some pupils she brought them back to task with remarks expressed in a conversational tone. If this did not have the desired effect there was noticeable sharpness in what followed – she did not use threats but her remarks were pointed and crisp. With other children she did not use a conversational tone as a preface to more forcible expressions, because she appeared to know that they would respond better to more direct criticism. With children she knew as potential disrupters she quashed any misbehaviour very quickly, and would remain close to them until she was satisfied they were working. By her mobility she avoided making loud reprimands and distracting other pupils by disciplinary interventions – a strategy that Rutter and his fellow authors (1979) noted as effective in maintaining good classroom discipline.

It was in her interaction with potential disrupters that she came nearest to issuing ultimatums, but she did this carefully. She made it clear that there would be unpleasant consequences if she were not obeyed, but she avoided challenging the culprits. What she said conveyed that the consequences for continued misbehaviour were certain, but, as they knew what these would be, they could avoid them. She spoke in the tones of someone reasoning with reasonable individuals. Her assumption that pupils would behave reasonably in response to reasonable treatment underlay much of her success in classroom management.

Sometimes, of course, this did not work. When a pupil persisted with disruptive behaviour or continued to mess about, her response was swift. The offender was told to clear up her art materials and report to the head of house. This was her final sanction, not very often used, and one agreed with her senior colleague. She had thought out the implications of having to seek help from the head of house and its effects. She was quite frank about it and as she explained it, it was a reasonable step to take. She said that she would not become involved with a pupil in a confrontation and was not going to be involved in an undignified verbal dispute with a pupil who might be sustained in it by the presence of others in the class. She emphasised that as she did not shout at children or nag them unduly, but treated them with courtesy, she expected them to treat her as she treated them. If a pupil defied her and would not give way, she knew she could not make her, and she was not going to attempt to do so by use of threats or by being drawn into a confrontation that might escalate or become ridiculous. She did not think that sending a pupil to a senior colleague weakened her standing in respect of that pupil, or others in the class. She reported that when a girl complained to her that she was unfair when she did this, she had said, 'What did you expect? You wanted me to argue with you and you hoped to rattle me. You were hoping to show off, and you wouldn't show off when you were on your own with Miss White. You had the chance of keeping out of trouble and you didn't take it. You know I am not going to fight with anyone in the class'. [She did not mean a physical fight] 'You know the rules in here'.

Her reference to a senior colleague is worth exploring a little further. Teachers do not like doing this, because they have the reasonable anxiety that if they call on a colleague for help, this weakens their own authority. It is true that if the art teacher did this frequently her authority would be weakened – although it would be more accurate to say that she would not have much authority in the first place. It is no use for a teacher to attempt to establish her authority by repeatedly referring pupils to a senior colleague, but the art teacher's position was different. Her classroom management was secure: her attitudes towards pupils and her skills ensured that. In these circumstances, calling on a colleague for assistance was one of her resources which she would use when this was appropriate.

In their management of pupils, teachers are expected to be continually successful. Since this is so important to them, it does seem surprising that when teachers describe their initial training, so many of them do not seem to have spent much time in lectures or at demonstrations which focus on the skills that are needed to ensure effective classroom management. The idea that in a well prepared and well presented lesson disruptive behaviour does not occur is very prevalent on training courses. This is true, but it is not the whole truth. As one exasperated teacher put it, 'No one ever told me what to do when the chips were down in 4Z.'

Reliance on a colleague's help is a two-way transaction. The colleague outside the classroom cannot be expected to accept one side of the story and treat the pupil as if the events which were antecedents to her disruptive or non co-operative behaviour were of no importance. The pupil may have disrupted a poor lesson with an ineffective teacher who brings about her own troubles. The teacher who asks for assistance may be one of Jordan's 'deviance provocative' teachers – one who behaves in ways that are described later in the chapter. There has to be confidence between members of staff who are involved so that if the absent colleague points to mistakes made in classroom management, there is no resentment at her different assessment of the situation. This calls for sensitivity and frankness. However distasteful it is for one teacher to call on another for assistance, it is preferable to the consequences of the confrontation described in Chapter 6.

When the art teacher reminded the pupil that she had had the opportunity to avoid trouble and had not taken it, she demonstrated an important rule of classroom management – that the girl knew what to expect if she persisted in her misbehaviour. Having made up her mind where her limits were, and being clear about what she would do in critical situations, the art teacher stuck to her procedures. She also illustrated a point that Dreikurs makes.

He suggests that as some pupils are set on a power struggle with the teacher to gain recognition, this inappropriate way of gaining recognition is best prevented by denying them the opportunity for it (Dreikurs, 1968). In some circumstances this may not be possible, but, as with a confrontation, it is better if a teacher has the initiative in deciding whether it would serve any useful purpose.

In talking to the girl who taxed her with sending her to see the head of house, the art teacher showed that she was ready to talk seriously about a serious matter, and listen to what the girl said. This was showing a good model of adult behaviour. In the same way, by her avoidance of angry confrontations she steered clear of any possibility that, in the heat of the moment, she would say or do something which was incompatible with the standards she set herself.

In some ways the art teacher better illustrated the attitudes and skills of the 'deviance insulative' teacher than the maths teacher. With him problems of management did not arise, at least as far as observation went. They may have done when he began teaching, but if they did, he must have developed and refined management techniques which he found effective. In the art teacher's lesson, it was possible to see the beginnings of disruptive behaviour which she insulated and extinguished.

THE DISRUPTIVE TEACHER

One difference between the geography teacher and the maths and art teachers was obvious at the beginning of his lesson. The pupils were not allowed to go straight into his classroom, even if there was no other class in it. They had to line up outside in the corridor, in straight lines, two by two. This is what many teachers do and in itself it is not poor practice. But with the geography teacher, negative interchanges between him and the pupils began with this. Waiting quietly was not enough; they could not enter the room until there was silence. This sometimes took four or five minutes, and what he did not realise was that it gave some intrepid spirits an excellent opportunity to trick him into some kind of game. They would shelter behind taller pupils and make just enough noise to prevent their entry into the classroom, but not enough to be detected and punished. Indeed many of the interchanges between the teacher and his classes took the form of ritualised games like this one. Inevitably the period of waiting was

a negative introduction to the lesson. It was frequently compounded by his poor time keeping. If there was a class inside the
room, it did not emerge when the bell rang because the lesson had
not ended. When they did come out the temptation to take
advantage of the crowded corridor was too much for the less
well-behaved pupils. Thus, even before the lesson began there
were opportunities for unruly behaviour.

When the lesson did begin, some pupils who had been criticised
for their behaviour outside the room were already in trouble for
delaying it. It was not long before further interruptions prevented
some pupils from starting work, and another ritual began. As the
pupils had to draw maps on some occasions, the rule was that their
hands should be clean every time they came. Any pupil whose
hands were not clean enough was sent outside to wash them. This
was well known and boys played the game according to the rules.
Once in the toilets the rule was to stay as long as possible and have
as much enjoyment as the environment could provide. Those who
had been noisy outside the classroom, and whose hands were not
clean enough to participate in the lesson, were criticised twice
within ten minutes, and they had discovered that they need not do
any work at all for about a quarter of an hour. There were other
opportunities for delaying or interrupting the progress of the
lesson. When atlases or paper had to be given out, he would say
'Monitors, give out the atlases.' The fact that he was not sure who
these monitors were would not have mattered, but with a strange
kind of perversity he would then ask 'Who are the monitors?' This
led to the sort of wrangles which frequently arise in badly
organised classes, and gave opportunity for further criticism.
When the work of copying maps got under way, he would walk
around the class as the maths and art teacher did, but his
comments on the work he saw were frequently challenging or
negative. They varied more according to his perceptions of pupils
than to the work that he saw. For those children whom he found
acceptable he would express mild criticism or emphatic praise. For
those he thought were 'dim' or 'miserable specimens' he would
express his criticisms which were pointed and often sarcastic.
These pupils were very rarely encouraged with any praise.

A noticeable feature of the geography teacher's behaviour was
his attachment to the long pointer which he used to point out
features of maps and diagrams. He did not put the pointer aside
when he had done this, but carried it around the room with him.

He never used it to punish any pupil but he used it to point at them, and as he walked round the class, he would turn the pages of their books with it. In their criticisms of him the pupils said how they resented this because it intimidated them, and how they resented his sarcasm and his insistence upon unreal and unnecessarily high standards of behaviour and conformity. He insisted on silence rather than quiet, he would overlook a raised hand in answer to a question if it was not held up perpendicularly and kept still. The effect of all this attention to detail was that a great deal of time was wasted in lessons. The frequent hold ups while he 'sorted someone out' added to the air of frustration in the room. He was very skilled in his use of the chalkboard, and his maps that he drew to illustrate points in the lesson were clear and attractive, but with that perversity which spoiled so much of his teaching, drawing them meant that he turned his back on the class too frequently with consequences which can be imagined. The prevailing atmosphere in the class was one of irritation and frustration. It was not surprising that so many of his lessons over-ran the time allotted.

Inevitably he provoked confrontations. His demeanour and physique prevented these from escalating to the point where he was likely to be challenged, but there were unpleasant incidents which he overcame by peremptorily dispatching a pupil from the room. He would not push any confrontation too far, for he had considerable skill at disengaging at the point of crisis, going to the door, opening it, and pointing to the corridor. This was the signal for the pupil concerned to leave the room, which he or she did without further protest. It seemed that the lessons were such that no pupil minded much whether they stayed or left them. This indifference was expressed by the third and fourth year pupils – they did not think he was worth their while. The younger pupils did not bear him any further ill will if they were ordered from the room. They had gone through the rituals of confronting him and accepted the outcome.

The geography teacher strongly believed in an adversarial approach to discipline. He saw it as a contest which he had to win – a characteristic of 'deviance provocative' teachers. This belief is not uncommon and stems from an incorrect understanding of what discipline is. It is confused with order, obedience, conformity or the results of a training which ensures submission. But it is more than these. It is inseparable from other classroom processes and particularly with the quality of the relationships between teachers and pupils. Discipline is frequently spoken of as if it were a commodity, something which some teachers have in their possession and others have not. When teachers say, 'He has no discipline,' or 'She should exert more discipline,' they contribute to the notion of discipline as a commodity. This misperception of what discipline means is well illustrated by the teacher who said that he was in charge of discipline in the third and fourth years of a school. But no one can be in charge of discipline in that way, as if it were the footballs or the visual aids equipment. When discipline breaks down, the break down is in the relationships between those in authority and those who are subject to it so that there is no common subscription to its processes and goals.

Two features of the geography teacher's classroom management are worth further consideration. He was correct in his insistence on quietness, of having clean hands, and of orderly behaviour. But his efforts to secure these were spoiled by his negative attitudes to pupils, by his conviction that they would not willingly meet his requirements unless nagged and hustled into obedience. Much of what he wanted them to do they would have done anyway if he had not been so sarcastic and overbearing, and ready to criticise them if they were slow to comply. In his complaint that pupils did not behave as they should, or learn without his constant goading, he did not see that he actively prevented the behaviour and learning he wanted. He managed, after a fashion, the confrontations he brought about, but he did not realise that each one diminished his standing in the pupils' eyes, nor did he take into account the uselessness of them. They tended to recur with the same pupils with all the wasted time and interruptions they involved.

For those who believe that 'good teachers are born, not made' the successes of the maths and the art teachers would be attributed to their personalities, or their charisma. When charismatic teachers are observed it is noticeable that they enjoy what they are doing. They do not only enjoy teaching their subject, they enjoy being with pupils, and they understand what they can accomplish when their relationships are mutually satisfying. And they deploy skills and techniques which can be identified – there is nothing mysterious about their success. Both the maths and the art teacher provided a classroom environment which gave the pupils cues for the behaviour and learning they wanted. Their classroom practice fulfilled those conditions, on which, in the view of HMI, a positive and appropriate classroom ethos depends. They listed these conditions: clarity about expectations; children's obedience to a sensible and fully understood code of behaviour; a combination of firmness and kindness; an expectation of courtesy; warmth and humour in relationships; sensitivity towards children's strengths and weaknesses (HMI, 1986).

When this positive ethos is established in a classroom, it is more difficult for pupils to become disruptive than it is if there are features present, such as resentment, frustration, uncertainty and boredom, which are on hand for them to mobilise or exploit. In the maths and art lessons, such pupils would not be given these advantages. In the geography lessons they would be able to help themselves to any or all of them.

Part III

Modification

Chapter 8

Rewards and punishments

Implicitly or explicitly, all teachers use rewards and punishments. Even teachers who would vehemently reject the idea of giving prizes use praise, affection and attention in a rewarding way, and withdrawal of such favours can be as punishing, in its own way, as a hearty smack.

To use rewards and punishments effectively requires knowledge and judicious application of the principles of behaviour modification. Aid available from studies in this area may be rejected by teachers who consider this approach to be manipulative and mechanistic. There is an unfortunate impression that behavioural psychologists are invariably white-coated scientists, most used to doing unpleasant things to helpless laboratory rats and inclined to treat people the same way. Even when not perceived in this unfair and unfavourable light, behaviourism is seen as a complicated, time-consuming business, heavily dependent on stop-watch, clipboard and technical jargon. Although many accounts of behavioural modification with children are written as academic papers by psychologists for psychologists, their implications are none the less relevant to teachers. Approached with common sense, they provide useful guidance on the application of rewards and punishments in the classroom.

Essentially, the behavioural approach argues that the single most important factor in learning a behaviour is what happens immediately following that behaviour. Pleasant consequences are most likely to reinforce the behaviour and make it more likely to happen again. For teachers, this means defining what they want children to do, then organising classroom events so that pleasant consequences follow when they do it.

Wallace and Kauffman (1978) emphasise the importance of

having a planned rather than haphazard programme for this 'systematic arrangement of environmental events which produces a specific change in observable behaviour'. The key words here are 'systematic', 'specific', and 'observable' and, though much will depend on a particular situation, the basic elements of a behaviour-modification approach to group or individual management will always involve description, observation, reward and evaluation.

DESCRIPTION

Most teachers' ideas of the behaviour they want their pupils to display start with rather vague constructs such as 'working hard' or 'not disturbing others'. Before thinking about how to provide pleasant consequences for these behaviours, it is necessary for teachers and class to understand precisely what the required behaviour is. In other words, to know what observable activities constitute the occasion for reward.

'Working', for example, might be defined in terms of a list of activities such as listening to, looking at or answering questions from the teacher, writing answers in a book or following instructions from the chalkboard. 'Not disturbing others' might be classified as refraining from such activities as grabbing, knocking over or destroying other children's books, assignments or equipment, calling out, pushing, scraping or banging desks.

Whether working with groups or individuals, it is important not only to be specific about the description of desired and undesired behaviour, but also to be realistic about how much can be achieved. Success is more likely to be achieved if a few problems are tackled at a time, rather than trying to apply the strategy to a variety of different behaviours. Thus, for a class, there might be few simple rules or conventions, observation of which will be rewarded. With an individual, however many and varied his problems, treatment should focus on one or two items, selected as being most critical.

Another aspect of describing and defining behaviour is the need to accentuate the positive by placing emphasis on the performance of good behaviour, rather than the avoidance of bad. Attention should not be drawn to anti-social activities by offering children a reward for not doing them. It is much better to reward some worthwhile behaviour incompatible with the cause of annoyance. Praise should be given for raising the hand and waiting for permission to speak, rather than requests made for children not to call out. When faced by children doing something which they do not want, teachers should ask themselves: 'what would I like them to do instead?'

Consistently attending to desired behaviour, while ignoring undesired behaviour, is a simple but highly effective demonstration of this approach. Not reacting to a nuisance is rarely enough on its own, because the other children will attend, even if the teacher does not. Providing a more acceptable means of giving attention is an important aspect of selecting a 'target' behaviour. However, it is always worth considering whether misbehaviour is important enough to warrant intervention. Teachers should ask themselves just what will happen if they merely ignore the source of the trouble. Frequently, the reaction of the members of the class will be the most crucial factor.

If it is decided that 'planned ignoring' will not be enough, then in choosing a target behaviour that will be encouraged, teachers should seek something that will contribute to academic or social adjustment. Usually this will involve providing some specific work to do.

Description therefore involves describing precisely what is causing the problem and exactly what would alleviate it. After defining 'what' is happening, the next question is 'how often' does it happen.

OBSERVATION

Some teachers experience difficulty in accepting a behavioural approach, because of its apparent insistence on a highly technical system of recording. Again, this reflects the origin of much of the literature as scientific reports on tightly controlled experiments. The jargon of interval recording and percentage rates per minute does make the whole business sound more complicated than need be. It is not that these techniques are intrinsically difficult, but, particularly when associated with timers, logs, charts and graphs, they do seem likely to introduce an undue additional amount of paraphernalia into a teacher's busy life. There is little enough time for lesson planning, preparation of materials and marking work, yet some measurement is essential if progress is to be monitored.

The simplest and most useful measure is counting how frequently something happens in each lesson. Obviously, as with describing and defining behaviours, it is best to concentrate attention in this case on one or two individuals or actions. This will provide a 'baseline' or starting line indicating, say, how often a child calls out or how many times desk lids are banged before treatment is commenced. This data can then be used to check the effectiveness or otherwise of whatever reinforcement is given.

Even before treatment starts, measurement can be useful in providing information about the nature of a problem. Is it sufficiently serious to merit outside help in the form of disciplinary support for the teacher or therapeutic guidance for the child? If so, it will help attract the assistance if the teacher can indicate the number of times other children have been hit, the frequency of interruptions per lesson or the amount of unfinished work.

Often the act of counting misbehaviours will itself provide either reassurance that the problem is not as bad as it seemed or an explanation of what might appear to be irrational or unpredictable behaviour. It may be revealed that apparently constant fighting only occurs with one or two children who incite these outbursts by provocative teasing. Seemingly senseless calling out may, on closer examination, be clearly designed to break the flow of the lesson and irritate the teacher. Assumed laziness may be related to genuine lack of competence or understanding in tackling certain subjects. In each case, there is still a problem to be resolved, but its dimension becomes clearly more manageable.

Sometimes objective recording will demonstrate that the problem was not nearly so bad as it felt subjectively. Actually finding out how often misbehaviour or distraction does really occur helps teachers maintain a sense of proportion. Young teachers are especially likely to exaggerate the importance of comparatively minor incidents. Defining and counting particular misbehaviours can demonstrate that these do not amount to a serious challenge to authority.

Another welcome side-effect of 'baseline data collection' is the way that sometimes the very act of recording produces a modification in behaviour. Gnagey (1981) recounts the story of a teacher who designed an experiment to stop children slouching in their seats. She started to mark down each time a child slipped down in a seat. By the second day the class had cottoned on to the fact that sitting up straight was important to this teacher and 'slouching' had virtually ceased. It was a collapse of the stout experimenter, perhaps, but this anecdote illustrates an effect which is welcome in the classroom, if not in the laboratory or clinic. Although it detracts from experimental validity, awareness that behaviour is being observed and recorded may well have an immediate beneficial effect. As Gnagey concludes, 'regardless of the horror stories you may have heard about students defying teachers, most pupils will do what you ask of them if it is clear and reasonable'.

REWARD

Traditionally, school discipline has been more concerned with punishment than reward. It is not surprising, therefore, that some teachers feel a system of discipline based primarily on positive reinforcement is a sign of weakness, if not an admission of defeat. Others would argue that, if not yet ready to love learning for its own sake, pupils should be sufficiently motivated by respect or liking for their teacher.

Perhaps because much of its basis in research has been concerned with extremely disturbed or retarded behaviour, positive reinforcement is seen only in terms of immediate tangible reward, inappropriate to the normal classroom. However, Neisworth and Smith (1973) describe a reinforcement hierarchy which descends from self-generated satisfaction, such as pride in a job well done, through self-managed reinforcement, such as going out for the evening only after homework has been completed, to the management or reinforcement by others, intangibly in the form of social approval or praise or tangibly in the form of sweets, money or permission to take part in some enjoyed activity.

Positive reinforcement can be seen as a series of activities directed towards developing self-control and working upwards through this hierarchy. Although aiming towards self-management and working for motives of self-esteem, with children the starting point is usually making praise contingent on socially approved behaviours. From this level, it may be necessary to resort to more tangible rewards, not out of desperation, but out of recognition that this is the most effective way to get rapid results.

Positive reinforcement occurs when the events that follow a behaviour strengthen its frequency, duration or intensity. It is thus what happens following the administration of a reinforcer, which determines whether it is positive. Whatever the teacher's intention, if the desired behaviour is not increased, then the reward is insufficiently motivating. Teachers may provide what they consider to be a variety of pleasant consequences for good work, but the quantity and quality of that work will not improve unless the pupils share the teachers' view of the desirability of the offered reward. Choosing appropriate rewards and a suitable system for their delivery are the most difficult aspects of behaviour modification in the classroom. Two techniques which help are the system of 'token economy' for groups and 'contingency contracting' for individuals.

Token economies

In the real world, money is a token which is later exchanged for goods or services; similarly, points or stars can be used as tokens which, though having no value in themselves, can later be exchanged for more potent reinforcers. This system has the attraction for the teacher that it gives prompt recognition to good work or inappropriate behaviour, without the disruption to normal routine which could result from having to arrange an immediate reward. It also means that children who may be working for different incentives or towards different targets can be dealt with at the same time. A variety of 'back up' reinforcers can be provided, for which tokens may be exchanged or certain activities made contingent on gaining a required number of points.

Once again, it must be stressed that the teacher's view of what constitutes a 'potent reinforcer' may differ from the child's. Discussion with the class will often produce novel, but sensible ideas. The following items and activities have all been used as part of token economies, although their suitability will depend on the age-group of the children and their practicability in particular schools.

Food is undoubtedly a powerful reinforcer. Sweets, chocolates and crisps are certainly accepted with alacrity, even by older children. There may be reservations about using this form of reward, on grounds of dental hygiene as well as financial stringency. Fruit provides an alternative which is better for the teeth, if not the pocket.

Drink – in the form of access to adult beverages such as tea or coffee at break times – is likely to be a very effective reinforcer for older children. Its provision, together with fruit juices and possibly other soft drinks, can present organisational problems, but usually children will be only too pleased to manage this for themselves. The sense of belonging to an exclusive 'brew club' will only enhance the attraction of this form of reinforcement.

Discreet supervision is essential for this or other forms of 'club' activity which involve staying in the classroom at break or lunch time. Congenial activities, such as playing board games or listening to music, can all too easily degenerate into aimless messing about. This can lead to damage to furniture and equipment, which makes what was intended to be a rewarding and pleasurable session into an occasion for recrimination. If this can be avoided without depriving the teacher of some well-deserved relaxation, then 'staying in' can be a most effective reward. It is puzzling that many teachers still use the threat of 'keeping in' at playtime to try to make children work harder. In the winter months, older children will do a great deal to avoid the bare and uninviting playground.

Another pleasant consequence enjoyed by most pupils is the arrangement whereby some part of a lesson can be used for less formal pastimes. An example which might be appropriate at many ages includes being allowed to use particularly attractive and specially reserved art materials such as poster paints or felt tips. Another example might be access to a comic or magazine section of the class library. A suitable collection can rapidly be acquired with contributions from the pupils themselves or from the children of a teacher's friends who are often happy to bequeath a hoard of old comics which they have finally outgrown.

Privileges such as taking messages, tidying the room, preparing displays or other monitorial functions are usually valued by younger children. With older groups, the opportunity to complete homework in school time is highly prized. Depending on the attitude of colleagues, the teacher may need to limit this particular privilege to doing homework set by himself.

It is often not essential for tokens to be actually exchanged for privileges. It may suffice to make access to them available, provided a target number of points has been gained. The key feature of the behavioural approach is to make positive reinforcement contingent on appropriate behaviour. Therefore a token system must be regulated in such a manner that children are not excluded from a choice of rewards.

In some cases, a competitive element may be appropriate with prizes for the best weekly individual or team totals. Though often derided, 'house points' do have an effect, particularly with younger children. As rewards, house points can be linked to class points with an exchange rate geared to an appropriate amount of work.

All too often traditional house points are awarded in a vague and arbitrary way, which serves only to confuse rather than motivate. Children should know that when they reach a certain cumulative total of class points, they will gain a house point. What the total will be depends on the rating given to a house point in particular schools. In some cases it should be the equivalent of one day or one lesson's average work, in other schools it will equate to something more like a week's steady effort. What matters most is the fact that it can be seen as an attainable target for all children, rather than the preserve of the brightest and the best behaved.

The token economy is likely to suffer from many of the same problems as the real economy. It is therefore vital for the teacher to be prepared for them.

Inflation is not a serious problem, in the context. Children quite enjoy attaining astronomic totals, though these can be kept in check by having a fresh start at frequent intervals. This will also stop hoarding if reinforcers are being sold for tokens, rather than provided if targets have been reached.

Forgery and stealing are more likely to cause trouble. Both can be avoided by careful choice of the method of giving tokens. Either the teacher needs to keep his own record or to organise distribution in such a way that any irregularities can soon be spotted. It might, for example, be arranged that every ten red tokens are exchanged for a blue, every five blues for a green and so on. Though time-consuming, such systems give extra opportunities for linking praise with the award of points.

This process of associating or 'pairing' praise with giving reward should help children to learn to value approval as a source of reinforcement in itself. Indeed the points themselves may become little more than an amusement, which may be dispensed with or continued according to the wishes of the class. If a token economy is continued over a lengthy period of time, it is vital to maintain interest by introducing flexibility and novelty into the system. This might be done by having 'sales' or 'special offers', when the token 'price' of certain reinforcers is reduced for a limited period and offering additional incentives or extra prizes in particular weeks. On the production, as opposed to the sales management side, bonuses can be given for extra effort with double points for working after an initial target has been reached. On some days, extra points may be awarded for tackling certain more difficult tasks.

Introducing a token-economy system needs to be done in a sufficiently light-hearted and light-handed manner for wrangles to be avoided. Sceptical children and staff can be gradually drawn into participation, if they see others enjoying the activity. Discussion before starting the new approach can help identify suitable reinforcers and a format for the delivery and recording of tokens that is fitting to the age of the pupils and the type of school. Basically, token economy in the classroom should be seen as an enjoyable game, rather than a control system. If the teacher plays the game with enthusiasm, the class will follow suit. If the system becomes a heavy, rigid routine, it will fail.

Contingency contracting

As not infrequently happens in educational psychology, contingency contracting is an elaborate term adopted to describe a simple process. It means that an agreement is reached between teacher and child that certain behaviours or performances will be rewarded in a particular way. What have previously been uncertain events, such as the amount of work from the pupil or the response from the teacher, become formally recognised.

Contingency management can be applied to groups; for example, the teacher only dismisses a row of children, when all are sitting quietly. The main attraction of this approach, however, is for working with individuals, who will benefit from an explicit statement of the behaviour expected from them and the effect it is likely to have. In some cases, this statement can be accompanied by the formality of a written contract, stating exactly what the child and teacher will do and signed by both. In the normal classroom, a verbal contract will usually suffice. Although a written statement will help each side remember the terms of their deal, signed commitment ought to be reserved for important and exceptional agreements.

Although using this approach is a more informal way, the teacher can benefit from applying a principle that has been found to work in arranging contracts with more seriously disturbed children. Known as the Premack Principle, after the psychologist by whom it was formulated, this states that: 'Any higher frequency behaviour that is contingent upon a lower frequency behaviour is likely to increase the rate of the lower frequency behaviour'. In other words, more preferred activities can be used to reinforce less preferred activities. More colloquial expressions of this principle, sometimes also referred to as 'Grandma's rule', state: 'Eat your greens before you get your pudding', or 'Wash the dishes before you go out to play'.

Careful observation is needed to make sure which classroom activities are preferred, but if this is done, then some academic activities can be used to reinforce others. For children who enjoy reading, this might follow written work, or in some cases familiar mechanical arithmetic could follow work on more demanding problems. Where drawing, tracing or colouring are involved in lessons, these should usually follow written or oral questions.

Preferred leisure or recreational activities can be made contingent upon the performance of academic assignments; Homme (1970) suggests that such rewards need to be immediate and frequent. Particularly when starting this approach 'little but often' should be the guideline. In effect, there may need to be a whole series of mini-contracts establishing a routine that 'first you work and then you play'. However, although tests should be small and simple to perform, they should contribute something useful towards the child's development and provide him with a sense of accomplishment. Contracts should involve earning a reward for doing something worth while, rather than receiving a bribe for not doing something. In this way, the teacher is not trying to train acquiescence or obedience, but is aiming from the start to move the child from dependent to independent effort.

EVALUATION

No form of intervention will immediately resolve all disciplinary problems. However, behaviour modification should begin to have some effect within a fairly short period of time. Somewhere between five and ten sessions should be enough to provide information for the assessment and, if necessary, the adaptation of a particular programme.

Ideally, behaviour is specified and counted in the phases of description and it should have continued to be noted during the treatment phase. There is no real alternative to this way of providing sound evidence of success or failure; however, it is undoubtedly time-consuming and realistically might be reserved for dealing with the most intractable individual problems. Some factual record of the amount of work done or the number of misdemeanours committed is clearly needed. This can be provided by having a recording or observation session at regular intervals, rather than every lesson. One advantage of the token system is the way in which it provides its own built-in evaluation. If the system is working, then children are attaining or exceeding their targets.

In a broader sense, teachers also need to evaluate a behavioural approach in terms of their own objectives. Is the system making teaching more pleasant or enjoyable? Is the investment of time in behavioural engineering producing a good return in academic achievement and social competence?

PUNISHMENT

If positive efforts are not working, then it may be necessary to resort to punishment. This is an effective way of changing behaviour, but teachers need to be well aware of its unfortunate side-effects. Punishment provides an inappropriate model of behaviour. Children may learn that you get your own way by hurting other people and copy adults in throwing their weight around in solving personal problems. Especially when severe punishment is involved, aggression may be displaced and, though compliance in the classroom is obtained, other children suffer in the playground (Vargas, 1977).

There may well be emotional side-effects which can be more devastating than the behaviour which provoked the punishment. Anxiety reactions may cause children to 'clam up'. Mutual aversion can build up to the extent that positive interaction becomes impossible, and teacher and pupil become trapped in a series of clashes developing into a spiral of dislike.

Although punishment gets quick results, these tend to be short-lived. The punished behaviour may only be suppressed in the actual presence of the 'punishing agent'. This phenomenon is disconcerting for young teachers, who find that though heads and senior teachers support them by punishing children referred for misbehaviour, on their return the offenders rapidly resume their provocation.

Sometimes being punished merely teaches children to avoid getting caught. This can add to problems, and sometimes lying, cheating and even truancy may be tried to escape retribution for an initially less serious offence.

For these reasons, it can be seen that although punishment works, it does not mean that it should be used. There are also ethical and legal considerations concerning the use of harsh, intense punishment. Perhaps the greatest shortcoming of punishment is that, though it may stop a bad behaviour, it will not of itself start a good one. There are times when behaviour is so disruptive, persistent or dangerous, that it must be stopped in the interests of safety, security and sanity. Actual physical danger to others is a clear example of a situation where punishment may well need to be used. However, there are many less distinct areas. Some children do test how far they can go and the establishment of clear boundaries regarding tolerable behaviour will give security to the rest of the class as well as the troublemaker himself. There are also times when teachers find that certain behaviours, though not dangerous or threatening, are in Churchill's phrase 'something up with which they will not put'. Instant reaction is rarely rational, but it is sometimes right. Provided that teachers do not find this response being triggered too easily or too often, it can be considered as a safety valve, preserving mental health and well-being.

Aversive consequences

Punishment either involves making something unpleasant happen or removing some reward or privilege. The main problem with the aversive consequences available in school is the fact that they are likely to be administered some considerable time after the event and there is a good deal of evidence to show that immediacy is an important element in making punishment effective. Impositions and detentions are nowadays received so long after the precipitating crime, that appreciation of cause and effect is lost. Suspensions and exclusions suffer even more from the delays occasioned by necessary processes of parental notification.

For the classroom teacher, lines and detentions are the most unpleasant consequences he is likely to be able to impose on his pupils. As with positive reinforcement, careful observation is needed to see whether intended results are being achieved. If the teacher finds that he is giving lengthier impositions and more detentions as the term progresses, then, however unpleasant he may think them, these consequences are not being effective as punishments. It is tempting in such circumstances to resort to would-be exemplary sentences, but apart from the effect on the actual sufferer, imposing very harsh punishment only heightens drama and tension. Better by far to hold to the principle of imposing as mild a punishment as is compatible with the seriousness of the offence. If aversive consequences must be used, it may help to establish a totting up procedure rather like that used in relation to motoring offences. Three minor impositions within a certain period of time could lead to an inevitable detention, though, as with the magistrate's power to disqualify, the heavier penalty could be imposed for certain serious offences irrespective of the number of 'endorsements'.

The punishment most easily imposed by the classroom teacher is stopping some pleasant activity or privilege. Jones and Jones (1981) describe 'activity curtailment', as they term it, as a natural way of altering children's behaviour, 'used since time began' and requiring no special forms of record keeping from the teacher. However, care needs to be taken to ensure that the activity to be curtailed is actually sufficiently prized by the child for its withdrawal to act as a punishment. This form of punishment can be most appropriate as a group contingency. Missing out on storytime or part of the lesson reserved for quizzes, guessing games and other forms of relaxation can generate an amount of peer-group pressure towards behavioural conformity. Such tactics should always be used cautiously, because resentment can easily backfire and previously pleasant parts of the lesson can become bones of contention.

Response cost

If a points system is used, then taking points away can be an effective means of demonstrating that certain behavioural responses will 'cost' their performer something, in terms of reducing the amount of positive reinforcement which he receives. Two problems can arise, if teachers adopt this form of punishment. It adds to the complication of running a token economy, because the teacher has to monitor inappropriate as well as appropriate behaviour, and it can generate negative attitudes to the system as a whole.

The difficulties involved in administration can be reduced by having only a few clearly defined offences for which points can be lost. It can be argued that response cost provides pupils with essential feedback showing what they should not do, as well as what they should do. Discussing which behaviours should lose points provides an opportunity to establish the rationale behind the application of sanctions. Gnagey (1981) suggests reasoning matched to the cognitive level of the children involved can have a powerful influence on the effectiveness of punishment.

Negative reactions can be reduced by ensuring that deductions are made in a manner which is not vindictive or provocative. Though reasoning may be helpful in establishing the need for rules, moralising at the time when they are administered is not helpful. It is more likely to be interpreted by the child as 'rubbing it in' and therefore may ignite, rather than defuse, a potentially explosive situation. Used sparingly, response cost can provide an element of just retribution and fairness, which indicates the framework of security within which a more positive approach can work best. In general, it is best to give points to reward good behaviour, rather than remove points to punish bad behaviour. It is better to give a bonus for punctuality than to impose a penalty for being late.

Another form of punishment in which cost is imposed for mis-behaviour is 'time out'. This American term describes a procedure whereby pupils are isolated for a short period of time. It may involve physical isolation by removal from the classroom or sending to a quiet corner of the class. It can also take the form of social exclusion from certain activities. In theory, the child is being withdrawn from a reinforcing situation and the whole technique depends on the assumption that the lesson is sufficiently attractive for the child to want to rejoin it as soon as possible (Leach and Raybould, 1977).

In the ordinary classroom, 'time out' is fraught with procedural difficulties. Sending a child out of the room is rarely in itself a punishment. Corridors and cloakrooms are full of interesting distractions. Taking a child to the head ought to be an ultimate deterrent, rather than a tactical option. Bare, blank rooms or cubicles are rarely available and though improvisation with screened-off corners or carrels may be possible, this does not provide the complete isolation from reinforcement and involvement which is an essential feature of this approach.

The sheer drama, potential for dispute and disruption to normal routine may even be welcomed by children intent on serious mischief. Although it may well be effective with small groups in special circumstances, 'time out' does not appear to offer an effective and applicable sanction in the ordinary school.

Avoiding unofficial reinforcement

However stern the intended sanction, teachers need to be careful that its application does not produce unforeseen and unintended consequences. Unofficial reinforcement can maintain undesired behaviours even in the face of harsh official punishment. Excitement and status are more important to some children than any unpleasantness that may also result.

Pupils who find that they can easily provoke angry outbursts from the teacher may exploit this ability to undermine a teacher's dignity and authority. There are times when a teacher needs to express his anger, but there is a thin line between rage and despair; he may stimulate fear or only amusement and derision. Even if compliance is gained in the classroom, the trouble maker enjoys a certain kudos in the playground. Lessons can easily become battles of wits, and although teachers usually win such power struggles, these conflicts sap energy and sour relationships.

If punishment must be employed, then it should be administered in a calm and matter-of-fact manner, free from recrimination. It should follow a clear and unequivocal warning to terminate the undesired behaviour. If at all possible, this warning should be quietly addressed to the individual and accompanied by advice about what should be done instead. This mild reprimand may be sufficient in itself to stop the misbehaviour; if not, then the threatened punishment must follow. Repeated warnings lapse easily into ineffectual nagging. Therefore, before giving a warning, the teacher needs to be clear in his own mind that the behaviour is bad enough to deserve punishment if it continues.

Perhaps the most dangerous unofficial reinforcement is the way in which punishment rewards the teacher. If successful, it immediately suppresses the unwanted behaviour and compels the obedience of the child. Sometimes socially reinforced by staffroom attitudes, the teacher resorts more and more frequently to punishment, whatever his ethical views about it. Efficient punishment is habit forming. Once addicted, teachers will find it harder to develop a more pleasant and positive approach.

Part IV

Monitoring

Chapter 9

Teacher stress and teachers' feelings

In this chapter we shall consider teacher stress and the feelings of teachers who are working under stress. While concentrating on the classroom events which are causes of stress many teachers feel, we have to remember that there are stresses which teachers experience which have their origin outside the classroom itself. Some of these causes of stress are within teachers' power to alter, such as inadequate communication between staff, a management style in the school which results in the exclusion of teachers from decision-making processes which affect them, a timetable which makes unreasonable demands upon them, the absence of an appropriate policy for the management of behaviour, lack of clarity about school rules and their implementation, or uncertainty about the ways in which the school approaches the children's parents. But there are other sources of stress which teachers do not have the power to alter, so that their feelings of stress are compounded by frustration. These sources of stress include having to work in an unsatisfactory environment which is badly planned and poorly maintained; unsatisfactory heating and ventilation; inadequate storage space; lack of adequate funding so that materials are not available and equipment is inadequate; decisions which are made at local authority level which seem inexplicable or unreasonable, and lack of support from professionals whose skills are needed in the management and teaching of children who are disruptive or who have special educational needs. Stress may also arise because of the pace of change brought about by the 1988 Education Act and the demands of implementing the National Curriculum and administering the Standard Assessment Tasks.

Outside school there are changes in the familiar pattern of family life and family discipline, and changes in attitudes towards authority figures. Many teachers feel that in their task of maintaining reasonable standards of behaviour among children and young people they have lost their allies in the community, and that they are left exposed to unfair criticism of their professional performance.

While all these are factors which contribute to feelings of stress, it is the events in classrooms and teachers' interactions with pupils which cause them stress that concerns us now – what Esteve has called 'primary factors' in stress causation (Esteve, 1990).

There are two definitions of stress which are helpful. Kyriacou (1990) defines teacher stress as 'the experience of unpleasant emotions such as anger, tension, frustration, anxiety, depression and nervousness resulting from aspects of their work as teachers. In essence ... an unpleasant emotional state.' Lazarus (1963) writes that 'stress occurs when there are demands on the person that tax or exceed his adjustive resources', and he draws attention to 'the person's appraisal of his situation and the role of frustration, conflict and threat in producing stress'.

When things go well in the classroom, teachers do not experience unpleasant emotions, nor does the pupils' behaviour exceed their adjustive resources which experience and training enable them to deploy in ordinary situations, meeting ordinary demands. It is when pupils do not accept or respond positively to their management strategies which are usually successful, that anger, tension, frustration, anxiety, depression, nervousness and conflict, or a sufficient number of the unpleasant feelings arise, so that teachers feel stressed. Frequently it is disruptive pupils who do not respond to the usual management strategies and whose misbehaviour if it is outrageous or prolonged is likely to stir up strong feelings in teachers. Thus teachers' feelings about pupils who defy them, or challenge them and flout their authority, are worth considering.

TEACHERS' FEELINGS

Anger

When observing teachers, an observer can notice that there are many teachers who do not ever seem to be angry, even when they are provoked beyond what most people would consider to be reasonable limits. Such teachers may be blessed with an equitable personality, they may have learned from family models as they grew up not to get angry, but to control or dissipate the feelings of frustration or irritation; they may feel angry, but their control of their feelings is such that the anger does not break through their controls. The observer sees the imperturbable teacher, but he cannot know what effort or learning has gone into the imperturbability. But not all teachers are like that. They feel angry, or very angry, and look angry. They must control their angry feelings, of course, because the code of professional conduct does not allow them to discharge unrestrained anger upon the child or the children who have aroused it. One consequence of letting the anger go would be that angry words or angry behaviour would provoke angry responses from pupils. This is not an inevitable consequence, of course, because some pupils, more likely younger ones, are so over-awed by the teacher's display of anger that they give up whatever it is that made the teacher angry. This is why some teachers pretend to be more angry than they really are.

But sometimes there is no disguising real anger which teachers feel welling up and which threatens to break through their restraints. With the anger there is frustration, and after the expression of the anger, regret and probably anxiety and guilt.

The feelings of frustration are of two kinds. First there is the frustration a teacher feels because the child is not listening or not learning or not obeying. By this non co-operative or provocative behaviour, the teacher is aware that the pupil is not doing what the other pupils are doing and that with this particular pupil he is not succeeding in his professional task. This, in itself, is hard for teachers to bear. They are expected to succeed, sometimes in difficult circumstances and with difficult pupils, and success confirms that they are doing their job properly. Secondly, as the teacher cannot act out his feelings of anger, and give vent to the aggression that goes with it, he is frustrated in another way.

The connection between anger and aggression is made plain when one listens to teachers talk about their anger. They will say, that once they are on their own away from the classroom and whatever incidents made them angry, they want to find some activity which allows them to act aggressively. They would like to smash something or hammer something and so dissipate or displace their aggression. As they describe these feelings and the behaviour, which if they indulged it would make them feel better, they will say that they feel ashamed, as if they are admitting to feelings which they should not have. Sometimes they will mention their surprise that they could feel so angry, and they feel uncomfortable at the realisation that they have such angry feelings. Dunham (1984) relates how one senior and experienced teacher was appalled at the anger he felt about the behaviour of disruptive pupils and Dockar Drydale (1973) describes how badly teachers feel when strong feelings threaten their professional calm and detachment. Thus feelings of shame and guilt frequently go with anger, and as if this is not disturbing enough, there is self-anger at feeling angry with others.

For teachers, as indeed for other people who work in situations which are likely to be anger producing, some anxiety is also present. This anxiety is due to an uncertainty that they are going to be able to control the anger they feel, and teachers will testify to this. When talking to teachers whose anger has been aroused, it is not uncommon to hear such comments as 'I just had to go away from her – if I had stayed I should have done something awful'. One experienced headteacher who was bearing as best she could with an extremely provocative pupil, exclaimed 'Just go away – I do not care where you go, but go away and get out of my sight before I do something I will regret'.

Feeling angry at continual provocation, at intolerable behaviour, is not unjustifiable, it is not reprehensible. Although it may not help them in an immediate crisis, it is helpful for teachers in recollection of their anger, to remember that it was legitimate in the circumstances, and further, to recognise that anger and aggressive feelings are as much their own as their positive and benevolent feelings. The important consideration is that teachers, like everybody else, should know themselves, and also know that there are not super people, who, in situations similar to their own, do not have to struggle with their anger at times. This awareness and self-awareness, reduces the likelihood of their feeling unduly ashamed or guilty when they are angry.

It also helps if teachers think about what it is that makes them angry: it is easy enough to declare that it is a particular pupil and his behaviour, or it is constant interruptions to their lessons, or the noise of the class outside their classroom on their way to the science laboratory, or whatever. But it is thinking in more detail that is helpful in preventing or reducing anger, it is a more particular kind of knowing. A teacher may ask herself just what it is about the particular pupil who makes her angry; whether it is his appearance or his voice; whether his behaviour is really very different from the behaviour of other pupils who do not make her angry; whether she has ever said anything very positive about him, or praised him. She may ask herself whether the pupil reminds her of someone else who has caused her difficulties. It may be that he reminds her of herself – for it is not unknown for teachers, and others, to be particularly intolerant of someone whose behaviour or attitudes resembles those of their own which they dislike and which they have had to struggle to alter. It may be, if the pupil's age makes it appropriate, that it is worthwhile to explore why he makes her angry with him. It would be surprising if that did not lead to an alteration in his behaviour. Similar enquiries could be made regarding the interruptions and as to why the class is noisy outside. In many situations – though not all – there are opportunities to avoid anger, or to lessen it, if one is prepared to be proactive about it and seek to find ways of preventing its occurrence, a process which begins with thinking about it.

Anxiety, conflict and depression

A major source of teachers' anxiety is the apprehension that they will not be able to maintain discipline, especially if they know that there are disruptive pupils in their classes, an anxiety which is aggravated if the disruptive pupils are in classes they only teach occasionally. This lack of continuous contact with such pupils prevents teachers from establishing workable relationships with them, and it is the relationships between the teacher and pupils which are the basis of effective discipline.

If teachers are unable to maintain classroom discipline, this is a serious threat to their self-esteem. They perceive themselves, and are perceived by others, as being able to control pupils and they are aware that, if they cannot control them, they will not succeed in teaching them. Thus, failure in control is a double threat to their self-esteem. There is the humiliation of being exposed to a very critical audience – the pupils themselves – and there is their knowledge that their inadequate discipline prevents them from discharging their primary task as teachers. This threat is hard enough to bear if the failure in maintaining discipline and in providing good learning opportunities can be kept as a private matter; but it cannot be, for their humiliations and failures are public. They are obvious to the pupils themselves and they are known to their colleagues, and to the parents. Schools are anyway competitive places, and the competition is not only between pupils, it is between teachers as well (Freeman, 1987). There are few more wounding experiences for a teacher than hearing a friendly pupil say 'It is not like this when Mr Best is in here, sir. He wouldn't stand for this mucking about'. To add to the teacher's misery, he is aware that Mr Best's good opinion of his skills is crucial to his chances of promotion. Teachers' classrooms may be their castles, but they are castles within the hearing and the view of their colleagues, including those who are experts in classroom management.

Anxiety directly affects a teacher's performance. For the teacher herself, as Lindgen (1960) has pointed out, anxiety narrows perceptions and inhibits ingenuity and flexibility in meeting demands. Hebb (1972) comments that anxiety impairs the ability to make decisions and results in confusion in thinking and action. This is characteristic of panic and teachers who are overwhelmed with anxiety *do* panic (Dunham, 1984; Kyriacou, 1980). Thus, at the very time when a disruptive pupil or unruly class make maximum demands upon a teacher, anxiety reduces her resourcefulness and inhibits her use of effective management strategies. In Lazarus' formulation 'demands upon the person tax or exceed his adjustive resources' (Lazarus, 1963).

When teachers are anxious, they communicate this anxiety to pupils in several ways. It is shown in the ways they speak. They tend to give instructions in tentative or hesitant tones. This may be because they have not thought out clearly what it is they want the pupils to do – and this lack of precision itself often goes with their anxious feelings. It may be because they anticipate some resistance or lack of co-operation. This hesitant manner has unfortunate consequences. It leads to confusion because the pupils are not clear as to what they have to do. It gives the impression that the teacher is not altogether sure either. It also conveys the impression that the teacher is not likely to insist on them doing something that does not, by the sound of it, seem very convincing to him, and he is not quite sure what he will do if they do not obey or co-operate. Anxiety is also shown when teachers give a rapid stream of instructions without allowing children to comply with one before they are overtaken by another. This leads to confusion as some pupils continually ask what they have to do while others attempt to make the best they can of the muddle. These rapidly delivered instructions sometimes include those that cannot be followed because they are contradictory.

In their anxiety, it is noticeable that teachers tend to talk too much, so that pupils are irritated by the continual interruptions, either in criticism or exhortations. They seem to feel uneasy if there are noticeable periods of quietness and their interruptions are rarely expressed in relaxed or reassuring tones. Their own confusion and lack of confidence, to which Hebb has drawn attention, is reflected in what they say and how they say it.

Anxiety is also communicated through movement. In talking to a young teacher and hearing her describe the effectiveness with which the Head of the school tackled any disruptive behaviour, she told how impressed she was by the way the Head walked. She said 'He never runs, or seems to be in a hurry. He comes along with this measured tread, as if there were all the time in the world'. The Head's measured tread was not the only reason for his effectiveness, but the teacher had pointed to an important aspect of his interaction with pupils and his effect on them. His tread gave the impression that when things seemed to be going out of control, he was in complete control of himself, and was untouched by anxiety as to what he would do. Observation of anxious teachers shows that in their movements they indicate uncertainty, tension and restlessness which unsettles those around them. They hurry about, 'Running along the ceiling' as one teacher described a colleague whose anxiety communicated itself to him – they use exaggerated movements, they knock into furniture and drop things. The teacher whose anxiety compels them to talk too much is often the centre of noise in a classroom. The anxious and overactive teacher is the centre of unsettling movement and disturbance.

The teacher as a reassuring presence is important in a classroom – perhaps more important for younger children than older ones. Teachers are not the only ones under stress in schools, for there is an element of stress for children in their learning. This is particularly so when they are trying to master new or difficult material. In most classes there are some children who are easily distracted and who are themselves anxious about understanding what they have to do and their ability to do it. Their anxiety is increased by the teacher's anxiety, and they perceive that someone who is not in control of herself is not very likely to be able to control them. As their anxiety rises, many of them tend to act out their feelings of unease in disruptive behaviour. In the face of this, the teacher becomes more and more anxious and the negative circle is complete. Anxious teachers tend to bring on just the behaviour they cannot manage and particularly wish to avoid.

Inevitably such responses to a teacher's anxiety leave her feeling depressed, with loss of confidence and lowered self-esteem. This depression reduces her spontaneity and flexibility, and like anxiety, it prevents her from making imaginative responses to unpredictable events when they occur. Thus, whatever steps teachers can take to prevent or reduce their anxiety or depression benefit them not only by increasing their own comfort, but also by increasing their effectiveness.

REDUCING AND PREVENTING ANXIETY AND STRESS

Enough has been put forward in the first four chapters of this book to make clear an essential message about effective management of children. This management is inextricably bound up with other classroom processes which include making and sustaining good relationships with pupils, the implementation of a lively and appropriate curriculum, good preparation of lesson material, imaginative presentation of learning tasks and confidence in the unanimity among staff in implementing an appropriate behaviour policy in a school. Even so, there are occasions when a teacher is on his own in some crisis in his classroom and has to act quickly and decisively. In such a situation a teacher is apt to think that he is the only one who is confronted with some form of unacceptable behaviour, and is at a loss in knowing how he might proceed.

To help in relieving this sense of 'aloneness', it is reassuring for a teacher to hear how other colleagues have managed when confronted with an uncooperative or disruptive pupil. Here Roberts (1977) has developed a technique, which he calls 'Staff Problem Solving Groups', which is effective in the reduction of teachers' anxiety arising from management of pupils. He suggests that a group of teachers most frequently in contact with a disruptive child first agree upon some particular behaviour which presents them with the most difficulty. They then agree upon some strategy to reduce the frequency of this behaviour, discuss its appropriateness, put the strategy into action and assess its effectiveness. This shared understanding and agreed action is effective in reducing teachers' anxiety arising from the behaviour of a disruptive pupil. The group is supportive, because individual descriptions and suggestions are valued, and because the proposed solutions arise from frank discussion about difficulties all the teachers encounter. This frees the teacher from the demoralising belief that he is incompetent, or alone in his difficulties. It reminds him that solutions to problems may be found when these are looked at carefully and honestly.

Roberts has suggested that a teacher may relieve his anxiety by talking with a group of colleagues. Another effective way to reduce anxiety is to talk to one other person who knows something about his class and the pupils in it, and something about the teacher, the subject he teaches and his teaching style. Thus a colleague whom he can trust and to whom he relates easily is in a better position to help him than someone who does not have this information and does not have any comparable experience. For the teacher to derive most benefit from the experience of talking about his anxiety with a colleague, the source of anxiety must be looked at as honestly as possible. Thus he must be frank about his own behaviour in any disruptive incident – if that is the cause of his anxiety – and open about his feelings of anger, or frustration, of helplessness or disappointment with himself. It is not easy for some teachers to do this, and it can only be done with confidence if the teacher knows that he can talk freely without concern that his listener will regard what he says as an admission of incompetence. It may be that the discussion will reveal that he has made mistakes but, if this is so, the value of the experience is chiefly that he will be helped to realise himself that he has made mistakes. Making mistakes is the lot of all of us and making mistakes and avoiding their repetition is part of a valuable learning experience. The listener's part in the discussion is not that of a critic but of a facilitator whose non-critical stance helps the teacher to explore his own feelings and to recall skills that he has but has not used. The listener acts first as a sounding board so that the teacher finds his own ideas becoming clearer. It is a common experience when talking of problems to a good listener for us to exclaim, 'I see now where I went wrong', before the listener has made any comment beyond encouraging us to talk freely.

Thus the listener is not just passive. He is active in his encouragement and active again when he is able to suggest solutions that the teacher may be unaware of. He does this because of his experience and it is in this that a teacher's colleague has an advantage which a wife or husband or friend does not have. They may be teachers themselves, but they are not aware of the situation in quite the same way as a colleague working in the same school and knowing the same children as the teacher.

Alternatively a teacher may find it helpful to talk to another person who is a sympathetic good listener but who is not involved with him at all in school. Speaking from outside the teacher's world, and from a different perspective, such a person helps a teacher to keep a sense of proportion about his anxieties. When such a person has robust common sense, and has seen more of the world than is seen through classroom windows, even if his advice and suggestions need some alteration or working up to make them appropriate, he will do wonders for the teacher's morale.

Whoever teachers choose to talk to about their anxieties, and they do not have to restrict their listeners to any one sort, the important thing is to do it, and not to brood over problems. If brooding does occur, the anxieties have a nasty tendency to increase.

A teacher can reduce anxiety about the repetition of incidents of disruptive behaviour if he thinks very clearly about whatever incident or incidents cause the anxiety. In doing this it is helpful to review the incident as if there were a listener present who was not in the classroom and therefore needs to know exactly what happened, with a detailed description of the teacher's and the pupils' behaviour. The facts to be made clear are:

- What did the pupil or pupils actually do? Or not do?
- What did I do? Why did I make this response?
- What was happening just before the pupil did or said whatever it was that was disruptive?
- What was I doing then?
- In what ways was the disruptive behaviour different from similar behaviour which I have previously managed successfully?
- Is there any sort of pattern to the disruptive behaviour? Is it always the same pupil? Is it happening at certain times in the lesson? Does it come from pupils in close proximity to each other?

The benefits of sharing problems with another person, or of proceeding with self-examination in the way suggested, are twofold. First, facing up to a source of anxiety and steeling oneself, if need be, to look at it closely, prevents self-deception and makes for clarity. Sometimes feelings of regret or shame lead teachers to thrust aside careful exploration of an unpleasant incident. This is understandable, but it is not very helpful in reducing anxiety through tracking it to its source. Secondly, when a teacher reflects on pupils' misbehaviour and his reactions to it, or when he describes these to someone else, he will frequently find the clues he needs to account for the misbehaviour and for his reactions to it. These clues are somewhere in the actual transactions themselves, but during an encounter with a disruptive pupil or pupils, because of the rapidity of the events and because of the narrowing of his perceptions which accompany stressful situations, he misses these clues. This is borne out in many staffroom conversations that follow disruptive incidents, when teachers say, 'If only I had realised that . . .' or 'If only I had noticed . . .' and 'If only I had stopped to see . . .'.

As confusion and anxiety so frequently go together, one way to reduce the anxiety is to be as deliberate and purposeful as possible. In practice, this means that a teacher, aware of feeling anxious as he thinks of a lesson ahead when he suspects that difficulties will arise – or experience has shown that they will – should engage himself in active preparation. Such activity itself tends to reduce anxiety because it involves him in a task, and secondly, the preparation well done will go a long way to reduce the likelihood of difficulties arising. In this preparation it is most helpful if he visualises the process of the lesson. That is, he sees himself presenting the content of the lesson, what he is going to say and when he is going to say it, where he will stand or sit during his presentation, how he will manage the distribution of any apparatus or materials needed, how he will manage pupils' movement around the classroom, and so on. In this visualisation, he is, in fact, rehearsing the lesson so that when he comes to present it, he is familiar with it.

Together with this goes his attention to efficient self-management which Dunham (1984) and Polunin (1980) recommend as useful in reducing stress. To this may be added the value of following a well worked out and appropriate routine to guide his own behaviour. Experience shows that following an appropriate routine does not give opportunity for anxiety to become dominant and its effectiveness increases self-confidence. Whatever increases a teacher's confidence in himself, even in successes which follow from mundane tasks well done, reduces anxiety. It increases awareness of what his initiative and self-organisation can achieve. It may not, by itself, overcome all his problems, but it does prevent him adding to them through neglect of matters which he can control and order.

Teachers who have difficulties in controlling pupils' behaviour are anxious about losing their respect. While this difficulty lasts, it is certainly a blow to their self-esteem and they need reassurance that they are not going to fail in their primary task. It would be foolish to deny that pupils respect teachers who can control them, but it is a mistake if teachers who are worried about their problems of management, do not keep their problems in proportion so that in their anxiety they overlook what strengths they do have. The confident exercise of authority which Robertson (1981) so clearly describes, is not quickly acquired. Marland (1975) has pointed out that teaching is a craft. All craftsmen know that respect for their material is essential. A cabinet maker would not attempt to work mahogany in the same way as he works pine. No successful dressmaker would work with silk in the same way as she works with linen. The craft of effective classroom management does not depend upon the deployment of successful techniques alone – there is the importance of the respect of pupils based on positive attitudes towards them.

In this regard, Galwey (1970) and Harré and Rosser (1975) have provided some interesting evidence about teachers respected by pupils. In their conversations with secondary school pupils these authors found that while they certainly respected teachers who could control them, pupils did not confine their respect to those teachers who were skilled in this. They said they also respected teachers who:

- Did not shout at them, and were not rude to them.
- Did not treat them 'like kids'.
- Did not have favourites.
- Were humorous.
- Could admit to being in the wrong.
- Were fair in their treatment of them as individuals.
- Were not boring.
- Were not over strict.
- Did not show off.
- Did not waste time by insisting on unreal standards of quietness and conformity.

- Could express genuine anger appropriately when this was reasonable.
- Were conscientious in marking their work.
- Learned their names and remembered them.
- Did not ignore it when pupils cut their lessons.
- Did not 'keep on' when school rules were broken.
- Continually involved them in classroom activities and learning tasks.

For teachers who are anxious that their difficulties in controlling pupils will inevitably result in loss of respect, these comments are reassuring. They show that pupils who made these comments could detect positive attitudes in teachers, even when their lack of control was not what it might be. For those who do not have these attitudes, nor effective control, their difficulties are considerably greater, and, furthermore, they are unlikely to be able to count on pupils' forbearance. Such forbearance counts for a good deal when the going is rough!

Chapter 10

Helping colleagues cope

In writing about 'the quality school' Glasser (1990) draws an analogy with management in industry and argues that whilst productivity, in educational terms, depends on classroom teachers as the 'first-level' managers, it also depends on how well they in turn are managed by the 'middle and upper-level' managers above them. Just as students and pupils should feel good about the quality of work which they are doing, so teachers too should enjoy a sense of being valued for their competence. In Glasser's argument, any shortage of effective teachers is caused not by any lack of individual merit but by how well teachers are trained and managed.

This view is echoed by Bennett's account of the work of the Elton Committee of Enquiry on discipline in schools:

> Individual teachers and individual school staffs can make a considerable difference to the behaviour of pupils and to their educational attainment . . . with this optimistic assumption, morale tends to improve but there is nothing more dispiriting than the feeling that one is being swept along helplessly, like so much flotsam, on uncontrollable tidal currents generated in an uncaring society.

The Elton Report (DES, 1989) sought to recommend ways in which schools, local education authorities and governing bodies could create conditions in which fewer teachers took the pessimistic and more teachers took the optimistic view of their work. Bennett's comments underline the point that discipline is not simply seen as a matter of what happens in the classroom, but something which permeates the whole life of the school and is influenced by many factors in the community outside. However, the most valuable contribution the school itself, and what Glasser would describe as its upper-level management, can make is the formulation and development of a whole school behaviour policy. The following recommendations from the Elton Report are specially relevant in this context:

- Headteachers and teachers should, in consultation with governors, develop whole-school behaviour policies which are clearly understood by pupils, parents and other school staff.
- Schools should ensure that their rules are derived from the principles underlying their behaviour policies and are consistent with them.
- Schools should strike a healthy balance between rewards and punishments. Both should be clearly specified.
- Headteachers and teachers should avoid the punishment of whole groups.
- Headteachers and teachers should avoid punishments which humiliate pupils.
- Headteachers and staff should:
  be alert to signs of bullying and racial harassment;
  deal firmly with all such behaviour;
  take action based on clear rules which are backed by appropriate sanctions and systems to protect and support victims.
- Schools should not use rigid streaming arrangements to group their pupils by ability.

The necessary practical arrangements for establishing processes and procedures for developing whole-school behaviour policies and evaluating and reviewing them are discussed by Stone (1990) and Smith (1991).

Stone (1990) describes an 'entitlement' model based on the rights of an individual, with whatever learning or behaviour problem, to academic and physical access to the curriculum; to social and academic integration; to appropriate learning and counselling support from specialist staff if necessary to ensure progress. Each school will be at different stages of development in these areas of entitlement, so there will be different starting points for drafting policy statements on organisation, methods and resources for ensuring that needs are being met.

Smith (1991) likens the process of developing behaviour policies to the system recommended by the National Curriculum Council (1989) in its guidance on how schools should ensure the best possible access to the mainstream curriculum for pupils with special educational needs by checking that their needs are taken into account at each of four stages in the planning process: (i) the school development plan; (ii) schemes of work; (iii) learning environment; (iv) teaching needs.

In terms of behaviour policy the *development plan* specifies priorities, targets and resources for organisational change. Instead of schemes of work, the behaviour management would then focus on a *scheme of discipline* which sets out the structure of responsibility for dealing with incidents, actions and emergencies; which states school practice on rewards and punishment and which establishes a system for recording and evaluating their effectiveness. The next stage will be deciding on the guidance to be given to teachers on classroom management and providing a stimulating and encouraging *learning environment*. Finally school behaviour policy will define how the *individual needs* of pupils with difficulties in learning and behaviour will be met through providing additional support, counselling and guidance.

The advice which follows draws together many of the earlier themes of this book in suggesting how senior teachers acting as consultants or mentors to colleagues can help make sure that well planned policy is turned into effective practice.

UNVOICED QUESTIONS

Marsh and Price (1980) point out that when one teacher seeks help from another, there are certain unvoiced questions in mind. They suggest that consultant teachers need to bear these questions in mind when responding to a call for advice about classroom management.

Will you listen: really listen?

Good communication starts with effective listening. A colleague with a problem wants a fair hearing, rather than a pat answer. Too ready a response may be interpreted as an attempt to brush aside the teacher's own perception of the situation. Martin (1980) gives a useful résumé of the listening skills by which interest and concern are shown through expression, gesture and tone of response. Attentive silence can be supported by maintaining eye contact, and giving a confirmatory nod of the head at appropriate stages of the narrative. Often people are encouraged to talk by what might be called 'listening noises', such as 'Yes . . . really . . . I see . . . uh, uh . . . mm . . .'. By repeating or paraphrasing key phrases or sentences, the listener shows that he is following the speaker's line of argument.

'I haven't got the time to spend with one child' might, for example, become: 'The group is too large for you to give this child the individual attention he needs'. The listening phase should conclude with a brief summary by the listener of the speaker's case. This enables both parties to check that the intended message has been received and understood. 'You think that problems arise with this boy, because he can't read well enough to cope with the textbooks in your subject'.

The good listener should avoid finishing other people's sentences, guessing the outcome of a line of thought or interrupting. Rephrasing and summarising should be undertaken as aids to memory, rather than opportunities for advice at this stage.

It is much more difficult to follow Martin's undoubtedly excellent suggestions than it sounds, when advice is sought in a crowded staffroom rather than a formal counselling session. None the less, these are valuable guidelines for helping consultant teachers demonstrate that they are really listening and taking seriously the viewpoint being expressed to them. This is particularly important in view of the next question likely to be in the mind of the teacher asking for advice.

Does asking for assistance imply incompetence?

Teachers may feel that asking for advice about classroom management implies some admission of weakness on their part. This feeling is likely to be reinforced if a request for help is met by a glib answer. It is important, therefore, that a consultant teacher should be able to establish empathy with colleagues. Empathy requires the ability to convince another person that you know how they feel (Hanko, 1985). Many teachers who are themselves superb practitioners of classroom management make poor consultants or advisers, because they lack this ability to see things from another person's perspective.

A teacher who is already feeling inadequate and doubtful about self-image as a competent professional will not be helped by easy or didactic answers. Even when the solution is obvious to the more experienced teacher, the temptation to show off should be avoided, and advice should be phrased in a manner which shows respect for colleagues, by suggesting, rather than dictating, what they ought to do. 'Have you tried separating those two children?' 'How about providing simpler work for the less able children?' 'What worked for me was reading through the problem sums . . .'

Will you tell the boss?

Another source of anxiety, which may deter some teachers from seeking help, is the fear that word of their inefficiency will be passed on to a higher authority. A tendency to gloat over the disciplinary misfortunes of other teachers is an unworthy, but not unknown, characteristic of some members of the teaching profession. It is entirely out of place in any teacher acting as a consultant on techniques of classroom management.

In an area with so much 'ego involvement', a teacher wants reassurance that advice can be sought in confidence, without difficulties being further publicised. Head teachers may feel that they can provide this sort of private comfort and guidance, without it adversely affecting their overall judgment of a teacher's capability. However, there is an understandable, though doubtless unfair, suspicion on the part of junior staff that, in dealing with 'the boss', anything they say may be taken down and used in reference against them!

The consultant teacher therefore needs to be an intermediary figure, whose involvement will be not exactly secretive, but at least self-effacing with confidentiality assured as far as possible.

Does 'help' mean extra work for me?

Another concern, which may prevent some teachers from asking for assistance, is a natural unwillingness to add further complications to an already difficult task. Unless suggested remedies are simple and backed by support in their implementation, there will be a reluctance to bring problems forward.

Teachers are unlikely to turn for help to a colleague, if they suspect this will result in their being involved in an elaborate and time-consuming behaviour-modification programme or urged to read a long list of books on psycholinguistics. Initially, at least, the teacher with a problem is looking for relief rather than re-education. This may be supplied by withdrawing an individual pupil or providing additional help in the classroom. Actual intervention by the consultant teacher will be discussed further in a later part of this chapter, but for the moment the main point emphasised by this question and the next one, is the need for advice to be simple, direct and practical.

Can anything be done quickly, which will make a difference now?

Some problems will need considerable investigation before a long-term solution can be found. However, to the teacher seeking help, in-depth analysis matters less than action, which can make working with a particular class or individual child easier and pleasanter within the next few lessons.

Hawisher and Calhoun (1978) suggest that advice on immediate 'instructional adjustment' should focus on mode, time, space and grouping. The mode of teaching might be changed to allow more verbal than written work, if the problem is related to the expression of ideas. Alternatively, it might be appropriate to require more individual written work, if problems concern disruptive noisiness during discussion. The time allowed for completing tasks may be too short for some pupils or too long for the class as a whole. The workpace may need to be adjusted by providing a quiet corner or separate alcove for distractible pupils. Some children work better in pairs or groups than on their own, but these arrangements need careful planning and frequent review.

At this stage, advice is best framed as a series of alternative approaches, rather than offering a simple solution. This will help preserve the self-esteem of the teacher seeking advice by involving them in making choices and decisions. In effect, the adviser requires an agenda for discussion, which will provide a framework for gleaning further information and for giving pertinent advice. The following five questions and four topics should help formulate that agenda.

FIVE QUESTIONS TO ASK

Asking the following questions will help the consultant teacher frame a rapid response, which should lead to a prompt improvement in classroom atmosphere and teaching performance. They need to be addressed tactfully and not necessarily in this precise form, but taken together they cover the main causes of classroom friction.

Have you told them?

Has the teacher given instructions which are clear enough, explicit enough and frequent enough to make sure that all the children know exactly what is required of them. Slow learners especially may need reminding about methods of presentation and ways of tackling problems.

More trouble arises from confusion over what to do, rather than over blank refusal to do it. As Lovitt (1977) points out, once children know what we want them to do, they usually do it. Discussing the clarity of presentation of lesson content and instruction can be an important first step in providing useful advice.

Have you shown them?

Has the task been demonstrated and examples worked through, not only with the whole group, but also individually with pupils who are having difficulty? Some children will need additional help, even when instructions are clear enough. Often a technique or idea may be grasped one week, but forgotten or misapplied the next. Working through extra examples at a child's desk can often reveal the reason for apparently thoughtless mistakes.

At all levels of ability, some model for the way work should be set out and presented can establish what are the required standards and prevent misunderstanding. Unless they are given such a clear and concrete demonstration of what is required, many less able children will simply not 'see' what the teacher wants. Often teachers do not realise how many mistakes derive from disability, rather than disobedience, and discussion of the difficulty of tasks may be helpful.

Have you listened to them?

This question can be considered in two contexts. Listening can involve hearing children 'talk through' the steps they take in tackling a problem or it can involve inviting comment from the class as a whole on the way in which lessons are conducted.

At the individual level, problems in arithmetic, for example, can be revealed by getting a pupil to describe aloud exactly what he is doing. In this way, the teacher may find that the pupil is 'carrying' the units instead of the tens and an apparently wayward answer becomes explicable. In other subjects, discussing and amending 'draft' answers can prevent 'daft' answers by giving the teacher insight into misunderstandings and misperceptions.

Readiness to invite comment and consumer participation in planning and evaluating lessons is a way of displaying openness that is much appreciated by pupils. It must be undertaken with some forethought. Questions about lesson content should be specific rather than general. Anything that approximates to an enquiry like 'What do you think of it, so far?' will invite the now time-honoured response. However, questions such as 'Do you want another explanation of Boyle's Law?' or 'Were there enough examples of quadratic equations or would you like more practice?' can provide valuable feedback to the teacher on aspects of presentation.

Have you praised them?

The frequent use of praise is the quickest and most effective route to promoting a positive atmosphere in the classroom. Very often the reason teachers seek advice from colleagues is because a negative atmosphere has soured relationships with their pupils. They have become trapped in a vicious circle of complaint and criticism, prompting surliness and disaffection which results in further antagonism.

It is not easy in this situation for some teachers to find occasion to praise some children. Initially, it may be useful to suggest that easier tasks be set so that children almost inevitably succeed, giving the teacher an opportunity to 'catch them being good'. In this way the malign circle of reactions will be replaced by a benign one, in which praise and pleasure promote satisfaction and self-esteem.

Choosing activities which are success-prone without being so patently simple that the teacher's tactic becomes obvious is a skilled job. It requires judgment about the suitability of subject matter and the selection of lesson content, which calls for an application of professional competence in the area of subject knowledge, rather than personal management.

From the consultant teacher's viewpoint, this shift of emphasis is wholly advantageous. It moves discussion from an area in which there is a poor self-image as an inadequate class manager to one where there is a sense of confidence as a knowledgeable specialist. Advice should always be aimed at developing strengths, rather than revealing weaknesses.

Have you realised how good you are?

Colleagues, too, need praise. Teachers should be encouraged to see their difficulties within the context of general success. Whatever is going wrong with one class or individual, there will be other times and places where things are going right. Examining their own more successful lessons and relationships should give clues to adaptations needed in the problem situations.

Sometimes lessons which work well with brighter pupils do not work well with less able scholars, because the level of readability of materials is too high. Some classes run smoothly while everyone is kept busy with individual work, but present problems when pupils are required to sit listening to a lecture for any length of time. Alteration to the variety and pace of lesson content may provide the answer. Difficulties may often arise at particular stages of a lesson, and this might indicate that more attention should be given to planning that part of the lesson. It may be that lessons start well, but conclude badly. If so, what is making the difference? Very often it is simply the fact that the teacher has prepared the beginning, but not the ending of the lesson.

With most individuals there are periods of amicability, which may be upset by particular incidents. Examining these may show the teacher that certain types of disciplinary intervention are more effective than others. With some children 'planned ignoring' or attempted 'signal interference' may be a waste of time but 'interest boosting' and 'hurdle help' can avoid the need for possibly counter-productive punishment. Teachers may feel that with some pupils they just do not enjoy any periods of amicability on which to build. If so, then they should be encouraged to look at those pupils with whom they do get on and consider how far it is their own approach or method of dealing with the pupil which contributes to the success of the relationship. Can some element of this approach be transferred?

By discussing problems in a way which stresses what teachers do right, rather than what they do wrong, the consultation should become a positive and a self-enhancing experience and thus one most likely to be repeated.

FOUR TOPICS FOR DISCUSSION

Thus far the consultant teacher's agenda for discussion has contained questions related to what might be considered the general strategy of classroom management. Attention should also be given to what might be termed tactical aspects. Four areas of lesson organisation which may spark off conflict, particularly with less able children, are standards of work, provision of support when difficulties are encountered, the marking system and the use of rewards.

Standards of work

Are standards set which are related to the learner's competence? Are the teacher's expectations based on a realistic appraisal of what the learner can do? Sometimes specialist-subject teachers are just not aware of the problems that some of their pupils have with basic literacy skills. In schools where special needs or learning difficulty has simply become another euphemism for the bottom stream, it is often not realised that many other children in the average-ability band have specific problems with reading or writing or spelling which affect their work across a range of subjects. Other children, though reasonably competent in these areas and by no means mentally retarded, do not easily grasp new concepts or cannot analyse and understand them sufficiently well to store new ideas in their memory so that they can be retrieved when required.

Further help may be needed from the school's special needs or learning support teachers, in the form of individual testing, extra coaching or adaptation of materials. However, at this stage discussion can be based on questions concerning subject matter and difficulty of task.

Support provided

If difficulties are encountered, what sort of support is provided? Is help given quickly and as unobtrusively as possible? With some children frustration is not easily tolerated, and a stage in learning is rapidly reached at which 'can't do it' becomes 'won't do it'. Timely intervention by the teacher can prevent the development of this sort of confrontation. Early help during the practice phase of a lesson and branching group work are techniques which can be usefully deployed.

Sometimes, if it is too blatant and obvious, the support system itself can become a source of contention. Children can react very strongly against what they may interpret as an attempt to make them look foolish. Where teachers are aware of a child's learning difficulties, but claim that attempts to provide easier work or extra help have been rejected or abused, it is worth discussing with them the problems associated with such 'overcompensation'.

Marking

How are marks given and recorded? Are these a source of consistent and sometimes public humiliation? Apart from driving instruction, adults rarely meet situations in which they are faced with persistently poor performance on their own part. Teachers, almost by definition, have seldom faced such situations during their own schooldays. It is not difficult, however, to appreciate how easy it is for pupils to transform the old adage and decide that 'if at first you don't succeed, give up and pretend you don't care'.

Particularly when poor marks result not from lack of effort in a specialist subject, but from presentational errors in writing and spelling, they can be a source of resentment. Sometimes publicising poor marks can result in silly, clownish behaviour, as a display of indifference, on the part of children who have done badly. Usually the response is a less direct, but growing disaffection with the subject and its teacher, which is at the root of the problems which crop up at other times in the lesson.

Marking is essential for record keeping and providing feedback, so if success is not being achieved, some feeling of failure cannot be avoided. The ultimate answer might be in a radical restructuring of the curriculum so that steps in learning are so gradual that even slow learners can make error-free progress. This is obviously a long-term aim and more difficult to achieve in some subjects than in others. More immediately, discussion should focus on the possibilities of dual marks for skill and effort, concentrating on improving one aspect of presentation at a time, and relating marks to personal performance instead of class competition.

Rewards

The way in which marks are linked to rewards can be a crucial factor in determining whether a child retains motivation or what Weber (1982) terms 'momentum', even in a subject he finds difficult. What sort of reward system is used? Do all pupils have a fair chance of gaining rewards for industry, if not for excellence? Exclusion from whatever system of reward is used can lead to a feeling that it is pointless even to try. This may be accompanied by an affectation of disdain for rewards which are offered and disparagement for those who do strive for them.

If reward consists of praise or relies on the intrinsic motivation of interest in lesson content, then the contingent use of teacher attention could be a starting point for discussion. This could lead to an exploration of whether some children do need some extrinsic and tangible rewards as a first step towards rebuilding self-esteem in an area in which they are failing.

If praise is deemed sufficient reward, then how can the problem pupil gain a share of it? This may be managed by asking easier questions and giving him simpler tasks, though this should be done with subtlety or it becomes too blatantly patronising. If house points or some other formal recognition is given, then a scale linking them to defined targets of class work can ensure that all pupils have a chance of gaining some public recognition of their efforts. If possible, without drastically altering their structure, lessons might be rearranged so that more favoured activities act as reinforcers for less favoured ones.

MINIMUM INTERVENTION

Advice on changes should always aim at keeping interference with normal routine to a minimum. Heron (1978) suggests that whenever one teacher intervenes in the work of another, the principle of Occam's razor should be applied. This requires that the 'most parsimonious' intervention, hence the least disturbing intervention, should be attempted, and more drastic measures tried only if this is ineffective. In other words, try the simplest way first.

Thus far this chapter has been framed in terms of what might be called a case discussion between colleagues. In a sense, this talking about a problem at second hand with a colleague is the first and least disturbing line of intervention. Suggestions are made by the consultant teacher, based on confidence in the ability and competence of his colleague. Not all the points mentioned would be raised at one interview, but, taken together, they provide a framework for an informal advisory approach.

At a more formal level, senior teachers may perceive a need for more direct intervention. This might take the form of personal observation and guidance, through team teaching or additional in-service training. For young and inexperienced teachers, the best place to start might be with a reminder of basic techniques for classroom management. Indeed, as a part of their induction to teaching, all probationers should have some such course at school or local authority level to supplement their experience in initial training.

In general, however, in-service training is a lengthy and long-term solution to problems that are immediate and urgent. In looking for methods of intervention that will produce speedy results with the least disruption and without loss of confidence or face to the class teacher, the consultant should start from the premise that it is usually simpler to change the behaviour of the pupil than that of the teacher. The sensitivity and tact needed to bring about changes in teachers' performance is well documented by Hanko (1985) describing her work with groups of teachers.

Intervention with individual pupils

This might start by observation of the context in which learning takes place, then consideration of the content of material and, finally, the possibilities of conditioning behaviour.

Focus on the context would require an examination of the present 'learning environment'. It may well be easy for an experienced eye to spot changes which can accommodate difficulties by providing easier access to help, support or control. Seating arrangements might be revised to decrease distraction or increase contact with the teacher. Distribution of materials might be rearranged to avoid delays in starting work. Monitorial jobs might be reassigned in ways which provide useful social employment for potentially disruptive children.

In teaching, more than most activities, it is true that the onlooker sees more of the game. The pressures of constant interaction make it difficult for teachers to observe their own performance objectively. A third party may be able to give helpful guidance on mannerisms or inflections of the voice, which appear to signal unintended belligerence or unnecessary insecurity. However, the presence of a third party is also likely to change the behaviour of all participants in a lesson. With a senior colleague present, a teacher is likely to be unduly nervous and a class may be uncharacteristically constrained.

Focus on content should concentrate on identifying and reducing difficulties caused by inability to cope with material which may be too demanding. The presence of a second teacher should increase the opportunity to talk through problems with pupils, identifying which concepts are proving difficult to understand and which texts are difficult to comprehend.

Providing some immediate relief from pressure may be the senior teacher's main intention at this stage, but he cannot remain as a sort of permanent co-pilot. It is vital therefore that discussion of content should be based on a series of questions that can continue to be used as a form of self-evaluation, assessing difficulty, variety, alternatives, revision and questions strategies.

If changes in context and content fail to improve the situation, then the principles of conditioning may need to be applied to developing a programme of behaviour modification. This may be necessary because of the intransigence of a particular child. In this case, the presence of an observer can be a great help for the establishment of a 'baseline', deciding what are really effective rewards or suitable behavioural goals for a 'contract' or determining an appropriate rate of exchange as part of a 'token economy'. As a last resort, it may be necessary to confirm that punishment needs to be used to deter seriously disruptive activities. The senior teacher is likely to have access to a more effective range of sanctions in this respect. However, before this stage is reached, it may well be appropriate to look at ways in which class behaviour can be changed.

Intervention with a class

The peer group may frequently encourage problem behaviour by its conscious or unconscious reaction to the individual concerned. Often, it is more effective and easier to alter that response than to attempt to suppress the original behaviour by punishment. The approval or amusement of contemporaries is such a potent reinforcer that it can outweigh all but the harshest of punishments.

Advice should be aimed at suggesting how the teacher might

involve the group in helping the individual. Direct discussion with a class could be used to illustrate the benefits of making their attention contingent on sensible rather than silly behaviour. This may be linked with seating rearrangements in which the potential disrupter is brought to the front, so that the others are no longer tempted to turn round to look at him. It could also be used as an explanation of why one individual is singled out for 'contracting' to perform a behaviour which others do without reward. Teachers often worry about this apparently preferential treatment of wrongdoers. Other pupils do not usually complain about this being unfair, and indeed being taken into the teacher's confidence in this way may be sufficient reward in itself.

Direct discussion can also be the best way to launch a token economy. Not only does this allow children to participate in deciding what should be suitable rewards, but it should also help avoid the negative and uncooperative responses which might greet an imposed system. If a token or points system becomes a source of argument, it may be fatally undermined. This is less likely to happen if the class is involved in its inception. One or two recalcitrant individuals can be easily drawn in once everybody else is committed to enjoying the game.

Some teachers, particularly if they lack confidence in their dealings with the class as a whole, may prefer a more indirect approach to involving the group in helping the individual. They may use praise, tokens or more tangible rewards to encourage fellow pupils to ignore provocative remarks and irresponsible actions on the part of children who seem intent on disrupting lessons.

Another useful idea is the recruitment of a more competent and mature classmate as a peer tutor or teaching aide to help with overcoming difficulties in work and to show a better example in behaviour.

Intervention with teachers

There are times when it will become evident that problems lie not so much with the children themselves as with their teacher's lack of understanding, inappropriate expectations or inadequate training. One possible response is to provide a good model of academic and social management – either from the consultant teacher or other teachers becoming involved in team teaching.

Though difficult to arrange in response to a crisis, this approach might be seen as more of a preventive measure, with some portion of every probationer teachers' timetable being given to team teaching with more experienced colleagues.

Where troubles arise in relation to one or two pupils, consideration might be given to their withdrawal from certain lessons. This is often done in the guise of providing remedial help, though unless some specific learning difficulty has been diagnosed, this may be a misuse of that service. In other schools there may be a special unit or a teacher with a designated responsibility for looking after children excluded from particular lessons. Although this provides some immediate relief, withdrawal can rarely be a long-term solution. It does not in itself help the teacher to develop more effective techniques.

Another form of support, which is helpful when there is particular antagonism between a pupil and teacher, is providing backup by requiring the child to report after each lesson to a senior teacher. This might be seen as simply another form of punishment, but it can also be used to provide counselling and feedback to both parties. This gives the more experienced teacher the chance to check whether a colleague's expectations are realistic and to amend them, diplomatically of course, through discussion of the child's work and behaviour.

As mentioned previously, more formal in-service training programmes will also have a part to play. Either within the school itself or perhaps more effectively through the local authority advisory service, courses should be mounted which give teachers the opportunity to explore and discuss the wealth of literature and information about the experience of effective classroom management. Where appropriate, longer courses involving more in-depth study and research as part of an academic award-bearing course may be the next stage in professional development for teachers with responsibility for pastoral care or special educational needs. Any profession combines practical experience with a study of the theory which underpins it. We hope that readers agree that this book has provided a guide to both.

Bibliography

Bennett, N., Desforges, C., Cockburn, A. and Wilkinson, B. (1984) *The Quality of Pupil Learning Experiences*, London: Erlbaum.

Booth, T. and Coulby, D. (1987) *Producing and Reducing Disaffection*, London: Blackwell.

Braine, M., Kerry, D. and Pilling, M. (1990) *Practical Classroom Management: A Guide for Secondary School Teachers*, London: David Fulton.

Brophy, J.E. and Evertson, C.M. (1976) *Learning from Teaching: A Developmental Perspective*, Boston: Allyn & Bacon.

Brophy, J.E. and Good, T.L. (1974) *Teacher Student Relationship: Causes and Consequences*, New York: Holt, Rinehart & Winston.

Bruner, J. (1966) *Towards a Theory of Instruction*, Cambridge, Massachusetts: Harvard University Press.

Cangelosi, J.S. (1988) *Classroom Management Strategies*, London: Longman.

Caspari, I.E. (1976) *Troublesome Children in Class*, London: Routledge & Kegan Paul.

Chazan, M., Laing, A., Bailey, M.S. and Jones, E. (1981) 'Young children with special needs in the ordinary school' in W. Swann (ed.) *The Practice of Special Education*, Oxford: Basil Blackwell in association with the Open University Press, Milton Keynes.

DES (1989) *Discipline in Schools* 'The Elton Report', London: HMSO.

Dobson, J. (1970) *Dare to Discipline*, Illinois, Wheaton: Tyndale House.

Dockar Drysdale, B.E. (1973) *Consultation in Child Care*, London: Longman.

Dreikurs, R. (1968) *Psychology in the Classroom*, New York: Harper & Row.

Dreikurs, R. and Cassel, P. (1972) *Discipline Without Tears: What to do with Children Who Misbehave*, New York: Hawthorn Books.

Dreikurs, R., Grunwald, B.B. and Pepper, F.C. (1971) *Maintaining Sanity in the Classroom*, New York: Harper & Row.

Dunham, J. (1984) *Stress in Teaching*, London: Croom Helm.

Egan, M.W. (1981) 'Strategies for behaviour programming', in M.L. Hardman, M.W. Egan and E.P. London (eds) *What Shall We do in the Morning?*, Dubuque, Iowa: W.L. Brown.

Esteve, J. (1990) 'Teacher burn out and teacher stress' in M. Cole and S. Walker (eds) *Teaching and Stress*, Milton Keynes: Open University Press.

Ferguson, N. and Adams, M. (1982) 'Assessing the advantages of team teaching in remedial education', in C.J. Smith (ed.) (1985) *New Directions in Remedial Education*, Lewes: Falmer.

Fontana, D. (1985) *Classroom Control*, British Psychological Society London: Methuen.

Francis, P. (1975) *Beyond Control?*, London: Allen & Unwin.

Freeman, A. (1987) 'Pastoral care and teacher stress', *Pastoral Care in Education*, 5, 22–8.

Galloway, D., Ball, T., Bloomfield, D. and Seyd, R. (1982) *Schools and Disruptive Pupils*, London: Longman.

Galwey, J. (1970) 'Classroom discipline', *Comprehensive Education* 4, 24–6.

Gardner, K. (1980) 'Failure to read: not reading failure', in M. Clark and E. Glynn (eds) *Reading and Writing for the Child with Difficulties*, Birmingham: Birmingham University.

Glasser, W. (1969) *Schools Without Failure*, New York: Harper & Row.

Glasser, W. (1975) *Reality Therapy: A New Approach to Psychiatry*, New York: Harper & Row.

Glasser, W. (1990) *The Quality School: Managing Students Without Coercion*, New York: Harper & Row.

Glynn, E. (1992) 'Discipline is for the whole school' in K. Wheldall (ed.) *Discipline in Schools: Psychological Perspectives on the Elton Report*, London: Routledge.

Gnagey, W.J. (1981) *Motivating Classroom Discipline*, New York: Macmillan.

Good, T.L. and Brophy, J.E. (1980) *Educational Psychology: A Realistic Approach*, New York: Holt, Rinehart & Winston.

Good, T.L. and Brophy, J.E. (1984) *Looking in Classrooms*, 3rd edn, New York: Harper & Row.

Gordon, T. (1974) *Teacher Effectiveness Training*, New York: David McKay.

Gray, J. and Richer, J. (1988) *Classroom Responses to Disruptive Behaviour*, Basingstoke: Macmillan Education.

Hallahan, D.P. and Kauffman, J.M. (1978) *Exceptional Children: An Introduction to Special Education*, Englewood Cliffs, New Jersey: Prentice Hall.

Hanko, G. (1985) *Special Needs in Ordinary Classrooms*, Oxford: Blackwell.

Hargreaves, D.H. (1967) *Social Relations in a Secondary School*, London: Routledge.

Harre, R. and Rosser, E. (1975) 'The rules of disorder', *Times Educational Supplement*, 25 July.

Harris, T.A. (1969) *I'm OK – You're OK: A Practical Guide to Translational Analysis*, New York: Harper & Row.

Harrison, C. (1980) *Readability in the Classroom*, Cambridge: Cambridge University Press.

Hawisher, M.F. and Calhoun, M.L. (1978) *The Resource Room: An Educational Asset for Children with Special Needs*, Columbus, Ohio: Merrill.

Hebb, D.O. (1972) *Textbook of Psychology*, Eastbourne: Saunders.

Hegarty, S., Pocklington, K., Lucas, D. (1982) *Integration in Action*, National Foundation for Educational Research, Walton on Thames: Nelson.

Her Majesty's Inspectorate (1979) 'Aspects of Secondary Education in English', Department of Education and Science, London: HMSO.

Her Majesty's Inspectorate (1986) 'Education Observed: Good Behaviour and Discipline in Schools', Department of Education and Science, London: HMSO.

Herbert, M. (1978) *Conduct Disorders of Childhood and Adolescence*, Chichester: Wiley.

Heron, T.E. (1978) 'Maintaining the Mainstreamed Child in the Regular Classroom: The Decision Making Process', *Journal of Learning Disabilities*, 11 (4) 26–32.

Homme, L. (1970) *How to Use Contingency Contracting in the Classroom*, Champaign, Illinois: Research Press.

Hopkins, B.L. and Conard, R.J. (1976) 'Pulling it all together: super school', in N.G. Haring and R.C. Schiefelbush *Teaching Special Children*, New York: McGraw Hill.

Jones, A. (1984) *Counselling Adolescents: School and After*, London: Kogan Page.

Jones, V.F. and Jones, L.S. (1981) *Responsible Classroom Discipline*, Boston: Allyn & Bacon.

Jordan, J. (1974) 'The organisation of perspectives in teacher–pupil relationships: an interactionist approach', unpublished MEd. Thesis, University of Manchester.

Kerry, T. and Sands, M.K. (1984) 'Classroom organisation and learning', in E.C. Wragg (ed.) *Classroom Teaching Skills*, London: Croom Helm.

Kounin, J.S. (1970) *Discipline and Group Management in Classrooms*, New York: Holt, Rinehart & Winston.

Kyriacou, C. (1980) 'High anxiety', *Times Educational Supplement*, 6 June.

Kyriacou, C. (1990) 'The nature and prevalence of teacher stress', in M. Cole and S. Walker (eds) *Teaching and Stress*, Milton Keynes: Open University Press.

Laslett, P. (1991) 'Children, family and society', address to Luxembourg Conference, Luxembourg.

Laslett, R. (1977) *Educating Maladjusted Children*, London: Crosby Lockwood Staples.

Laslett, R. (1982) *Maladjusted Children in the Ordinary School*, Stratford upon Avon: National Council for Special Education.

Lazarus, R.S. (1963) *Personality and Adjustment*, Englewood Cliffs, New Jersey: Prentice Hall.

Leach, D. and Raybould, E.C. (1977) *Learning and Behaviour Difficulties in Schools*, London: Open Books.

Lemlech, J.K. (1979) *Classroom Management*, New York: Harper & Row.

Lemlech, J.K. (1988) *Classroom Management*, 2nd edn, New York: Harper & Row.

Lindgen, J.A. (1960) 'Neuroses of school teachers: a colloquy', *Mental Hygiene*, 44, 79–90.

Long, N.J. and Newman, R.G. (1976) 'Managing surface behaviour of children in school', in N.J. Long, W.C. Morse and R.G. Newman *Conflict in the Classroom*, 3rd edn, Belmont, California: Wadsworth.

Lovitt, T.C. (1977) *In Spite of My Resistance: I've Learned from Children*, Columbus, Ohio: Merrill.

Lunzer, E. and Gardner, K. (1979) *The Effective Use of Reading*, London: Heinemann.

McManus, M. (1989) *Troublesome Behaviour in the Classroom: A Teacher's Survival Guide*, London: Routledge.

Marland, M. (1975) *The Craft of the Classroom: A Survival Guide*, London: Heinemann.

Marsh, G.E. and Price, B.J. (1980) *Methods for Teaching the Mildly Retarded Adolescent*, St Louis: Mosby.

Marsh, P., Rosser, E. and Harre, R. (1978) *The Rules of Disorder*, London: Routledge & Kegan Paul.

Martin, R. and Lauridsen, D. (1974) *Developing Student Discipline and Motivation*, Champaign, Illinois: Research Press.

Martin, R.J. (1980) *Teaching Through Encouragement: Techniques to Help Students Learn*, Englewood Cliffs, New Jersey: Prentice Hall.

Meighan, R.M. (1978) *A Sociology of Educating*, New York: Holt, Rinehart & Winston.

Mills, W.C.P. (1976) 'The seriously disruptive behaviour of pupils in secondary schools in one local authority', unpublished MEd. thesis, University of Birmingham.

National Curriculum Council (1989) *Curriculum Guidance Two. A Curriculum for All: Special Needs in the National Curriculum*, York: National Curriculum Council.

Neisworth, J.T. and Smith, R.M. (1973) *Modifying Retarded Behaviour*, Boston: Houghton Mifflin.

O'Leary, K.D. and O'Leary, S.E. (1977) *Classroom Management*, New York: Pergamon Press.

Pik, R. (1981) 'Confrontation situations and teacher support systems', in B. Gillham (ed.) *Problem Behaviour in the Secondary School*, London: Croom Helm.

Polunin, M. (1980) *The Health and Fitness Handbook*, New York: Frances Lincoln/Windward.

Protect, J.A.(1973) *Behaviour Modification: A Practical Guide for Teachers*, London: University of London Press.

Raban, B. and Postlethwaite, K. (1988) *Classroom Responses to Learning Difficulties*, Basingstoke: Macmillan Education.

Raths, L.E., Harmin, M. and Simon, S.B. (1980) *Values and Teaching*, Columbus, Ohio: Merrill.

Redl, F. (1959) 'The concept of the life space interview', *American Journal of Orthopsychiatry*, xxix, 1–18.

Redl, F. (1971) 'The concept of punishment', in N.J. Long, W.C.Morse and R.E. Newman (eds) *Conflict in the Classroom*, 3rd edn, Belmont, California: Wadsworth.

Redl, F. and Wineman, D. (1951) *Children Who Hate*, New York: Free Press.

Redl, F. and Wineman, D. (1952) *Controls from Within*, New York: Free Press.

Roberts, B. (1977) 'Treating children in secondary schools', *Educational Review*, 29 (3) 204–12.

Robertson, J. (1981) *Effective Classroom Control*, London: Hodder & Stoughton.

Roe, A.M. (1978) 'Medical and psychological concepts of problem behaviour', in B. Gillham (ed.) *Reconstructing Educational Psychology*, London: Croom Helm.

Rosenthal, R. and Jacobson, L.F. (1968) *Pygmalion in the Classroom*, New York: Holt, Rinehart & Winston.

Rutter, M., Maughan, B., Mortimore, P. and Ouston, J. (1979) *Fifteen Thousand Hours: Secondary Schools and their Effects on Children*, London: Open Books.

Rutter, M., Tizard, J. and Whitmore, K. (1970) *Education, Health and Behaviour*, London: Longman.

Saunders, M. (1979) *Class Control and Behaviour*, London: McGraw Hill.

Skinner, B.F. (1968) *The Technology of Teaching*, New York: Appleton Century Crofts.

Smith, C.J. (1990) 'The management of children with emotional and behavioural difficulties in ordinary and special schools', V.P. Varma (ed.) *The Management of Children with Emotional and Behaviour Difficulties*, London: Routledge.

Smith, C.J. (1991) 'Behaviour management – a whole school policy', in M. Hinson (ed.) *Teachers and Special Educational Needs: Coping with Change*, London: Longman.

Smith, C.J. (1992a) 'Keeping them clever: preventing learning difficulties from becoming learning problems', in K. Wheldall (ed.) *Discipline in Schools: Psychological Perspectives on the Elton Report*, London: Routledge.

Smith, C.J. (1992b) 'Management of special needs', in R. Gulliford and G. Upton (eds) *Special Educational Needs*, London: Routledge.

Smith, S.L. (1979) *No Easy Answers: Teaching the Learning Troubled Child*, Cambridge, Massachusetts: Winthrop.

Stone, L. (1990) *Managing Difficult Children in School*, Oxford: Basil Blackwell.

Thomas, G. (1988) 'Planning for support in the mainstream', in G. Thomas and A. Feiler (eds) *Planning for Special Needs: A Whole School Approach*, Oxford: Basil Blackwell.

Ullman, L. and Krasner, L. (1965) *Case Studies in Behaviour Modification*, New York: Holt, Rinehart & Winston.

Vargas, J.E. (1977) *Behavioural Psychology for Teachers*, New York: Harper & Row.

Wallace, G. and Kauffman, J.M. (1978) *Teaching Children with Learning Problems*, Columbus, Ohio: Merrill.

Waterhouse, P. (1983) *Managing the Learning Process*, London: McGraw Hill.

Weber, K.J. (1982) *The Teacher is the Key: A Practical Guide for Teaching the Adolescent with Learning Difficulties*, Milton Keynes: Open University Press.

Wheldall, K. and Merrett, F. (1992) 'Effective classroom behaviour management: positive teaching', in K. Wheldall (ed.) (1992) *Discipline in Schools: Psychological Perspectives on the Elton Report*, London: Routledge.

Wilson, M. and Evans, M. (1980) *Education of Disturbed Pupils*, London: Methuen.

Wolfgang, C.H. and Glickman, C.D. (1986) *Solving Discipline Problems* 2nd edn, Boston: Allyn & Bacon.

Wragg, E.C. (1978) 'Death by a thousand workcards', *Times Educational Supplement*, 3 November.
Wragg, E.C. (1984) *Classroom Teaching Skills*, London: Croom Helm.

Author index

Subject index